LEILA LINDHOLM

a piece of cake

Over 200 of Leila's favourite, easy-to-follow baking recipes

New Holland

my kitchen heroes

I've loved baking for as long as I can remember. My Mum never missed an opportunity to tie aprons around us ready for a big baking session and my Granny was a keen baker too. I can remember standing on a stool in my grandmother's kitchen as a three-year old, putting a sticky mixture into muffin cases. The best bit was licking the bowl clean afterwards – I never missed out on that!

The best recipes are passed down, from one generation to the next being adapted, polished and preserved like family treasures. That is part of the magic of baking. I am not the kind of person to keep recipes secret. Why do that when you can give those around you – and yourself – so many happy moments with delicious cakes, breads and buns?

When I was young I was an honorary member of a baking club called the Muffin Mafia. It consisted of me, a neighbour, Aunt Elsa and a crew of other aunts. I'm not quite sure how many other members there were besides myself and Aunt Elsa – I suspect that my aunt started the club mainly for my benefit, and, boy, did I think it was exciting! The purpose of the club was to exchange recipes via letters (an early form of communication), which were then tested and entered into a charming little notebook. I used to rush to Elsa's at every opportunity, and there I learned to bake delicious muffins, bread, buns and sponges.

I thought the whole thing was fantastic, and looking back I realise how clever Elsa was to conjure up a sense of mystique around baking and recipes. For a small child (and probably for many adults too), it's almost magical to see beautiful and tasty cakes and breads arising from little more than a few eggs, a bag of flour and some sugar.

Baking with your kids or grandchildren is a superb pastime. There's something special about sharing the magic of creation. It works no matter how old or young you are, and for me it has been a lifelong romance with masses of happy memories together with friends and relatives. I hope to share some of this with you too. Some people say life is a bowl of cherries, but for me it's a plate of freshly baked buns and a glass of berry squash!

Bake with love *Leila*

in the cookie jar

It's not always easy to keep your hands out of the cookie jar. Those cookies look so terribly tempting standing there in the larder, and just knowing how they taste is enough to make your mouth water. Fortunately, many cookies and biscuits are at their best when freshly baked so the problem tends to solve itself through regular coffee mornings. Biscotti, on the other hand, ought to sit on that shelf a little bit longer ...

four different chocolate chip cookies

This is my favourite chocolate chip cookie recipe. You can make the cookie dough in advance and keep it in the freezer for a few weeks. Then all you have to do is take the dough out of the freezer, slice and bake! You can vary the recipe with all kinds of delicious flavours.

MAKES 25 COOKIES
BASIC RECIPE
125 g (4 ½ oz) unsalted butter, softened
90 g (3 ½ oz) demerara sugar
1 organic egg
90 g (3 ½ oz) plain flour
20 g (¾ oz) rolled oats
½ tablespoon baking powder
¼ tablespoon salt
100 g (4 oz) good quality dark chocolate (70% cocoa solids)
zest of 1 lime

1. Beat the butter and the sugar until creamy. Mix in the egg.
2. Mix the flour, rolled oats, baking powder and salt and blend into the dough.
3. Chop the chocolate coarsely and mix into the dough together with the lime zest.
4. Shape the dough into a roll 5 cm (2 in) thick and roll it up in greaseproof paper or clingfilm. Put the dough in the freezer for about 30 minutes.
5. Preheat the oven to 180°C/350°F/gas 4.
6. Cut the roll into slices 1 cm (½ in) thick and put them on a baking sheet lined with greaseproof paper.
7. Bake the cookies in the centre of the oven for about 10 minutes or until golden.

white chocolate chip ginger cookies

MAKES 25 COOKIES
1 batch of cookie dough, see basic recipe
100 g (4 oz) good quality white chocolate (instead of dark chocolate)
3.5 cm (1 ½ in) fresh root ginger

1. Prepare the cookie dough according to the basic recipe, but replace the dark chocolate with white chocolate and add the peeled and grated ginger when you mix the butter and sugar.

chocolate chip orange cookies

MAKES 25 COOKIES
1 batch of cookie dough, see basic recipe
20 g (¾ oz) desiccated coconut (instead of rolled oats)
zest of 2 oranges (instead of 1 lime)

1. Prepare the cookie dough according to the basic recipe, but replace the rolled oats with desiccated coconut and replace the lime zest with orange zest.

chocolate chip peanut cookies

MAKES 25 COOKIES
1 batch of cookie dough, see basic recipe
75 g (3 oz) salted peanuts

1. Prepare the cookie dough according to the basic recipe and add chopped peanuts with the other dry ingredients.

sugar & spice

Sugar comes from sugar cane and sugar beet and has different characteristics depending on how it has been prepared.

Muscovado sugar
Muscovado is a wickedly rich tasting sugar that is traditionally made from the sugar cane grown in Mauritius. In contrast to white granular sugar, muscovado sugar is raw, unrefined sugar, and it has a natural colour and distinctive flavour. It's taste is similar to demerara sugar but richer. The dark variety has a definite liquorice accent, while the light variety has a caramel flavour. Muscovado sugar is used in desserts, and it works very well with chocolate. It can also be used to make ice cream and in baking bread and cookies. My mum loves using it in Irish coffee. Delicious!

Icing sugar
Icing sugar is finely ground granular sugar with some added anti-caking agent to prevent clumping. It is used when you want to sweeten something without the sugar crystals being visible or felt. It is used in icing, toppings or to sweeten cream or yogurt. You can also dust it over cakes or desserts for a finishing touch.

Caster sugar
Caster sugar is the most widely used for cakes and pastries. It is made by purifying and refining sugar beet or sugar cane, giving it a pure white colour.

Demerara sugar
Demerara sugar consists of sugar crystals made from dark brown sugar cane syrup, which gives it a special piquant accent in contrast to the neutral sweetness of white granular sugar. You can use it for sweetening in bakery and desserts and also to liven up sauces, marinades and casseroles.

Vanilla sugar
Vanilla adds a special touch to many cakes and cookies. There are different kinds of vanilla sugar and the type I've used in many of my recipes has the consistency of icing sugar. If you can't get hold of it in your local shop it's easy to make your own. Just add a split vanilla pod or two to an airtight container containing about 150g (5 oz) of icing sugar and leave to stand for a couple of weeks. Alternatively, use a couple of dried up vanilla pods and mix them with about 500 g (1 lb) of caster sugar in a blender until you get a powdery consistency. Soon you won't be able to bake without it, and you'll never go back to using synthetic vanilla essence again.

coconut pyramids

This recipe is absolutely wonderful and you just have to try it out. The trick is to mix lime zest in the mixture. I usually dip the base of the coconut pyramids in melted chocolate and leave them to set in paper cases or on a wire rack. Coconut and chocolate are an irresistible combination of flavours!

MAKES 16 PYRAMIDS
50 g (2 oz) unsalted butter
2 organic eggs
90 g (3 ½ oz) caster sugar
250 g (9 oz) desiccated coconut
zest of 1 lime
1 tablespoon Amaretto liqueur or rum

1. Preheat the oven to 175°C/350°F/gas 4.
2. Melt the butter and mix it with the other ingredients.
3. Let the mixture swell for about 10 minutes.
4. Shape the mixture into pyramids on a baking sheet lined with greaseproof paper.
5. Bake in the centre of the oven for about 15 minutes or until golden.

french madeleines

These small, shell-shaped and incredibly tasty French cakes are almost as soft as mini sponges. You will need Madeleine tins or some other kind of small bun tins.

MAKES 12 MADELEINES
75 g (3 oz) soft butter
75 g (3 oz) caster sugar
1 teaspoon vanilla sugar
zest of 1 lemon
2 organic eggs
90 g (3 ½ oz) plain flour
1 teaspoon baking powder
butter and dried breadcrumbs for the madeleine or small bun tins

1. Preheat the oven to 175°C/350°F/gas 4.
2. Beat together the butter, sugar, vanilla sugar and lime zest until light and creamy.
3. Mix in the eggs.
4. Mix together the flour and baking powder and blend into the mixture.
5. Grease and coat the cake tins with breadcrumbs.
6. Spoon the mixture into the tins and bake in the centre of the oven for 10 minutes or until golden.

saffron biscotti

MAKES 35 BISCUITS

100 g (4 oz) unsalted butter
1 pinch of saffron
2 organic eggs
135 g (4 ¾ oz) caster sugar
300 g (11 oz) plain flour
1 ½ teaspoons baking powder
90 g (3 ½ oz) almonds

1. Preheat the oven to 175°C/350°F/gas 4.
2. Melt the butter and mix in the saffron. Pour in the butter into a bowl and beat in the eggs.
3. Mix the dry ingredients with the whole almonds and blend into the saffon butter.
4. Shape the dough into three loaves and put them on a baking sheet lined with greaseproof paper.
5. Bake in the centre of the oven for about 25 minutes.
6. Take out the loaves and reduce the temperature to 120°C/250°F/gas ½.
7. Cut the loaves into 1 cm (½ in) slices. Return the slices to the baking tin.
8. Leave to dry in the centre of the oven for about 15 minutes.

biscotti di prato

These yummy, crunchy biscuits originate from Tuscany, where they are often served together with the Italian dessert wine Vin Santo. The biscuits are dipped in the sweet wine just as we dunk our biscuits in coffee.

MAKES 30 BISCUITS

100 g (4 oz) almonds
75 g (3 oz) pine nuts
½ vanilla pod
240 g (8 ½ oz) plain flour
180 g (6 ¼ oz) caster sugar
zest of 1 orange
¼ teaspoon baking powder
1 pinch of salt
2 organic eggs

1. Preheat the oven to 175°C/350°F/gas 4.
2. Blanch the almonds. Toast them in the oven for about 5 minutes until they turn lightly brown.
3. Chop the almonds and the pine nuts coarsely. Split the vanilla pod lengthways and scrape out the seeds.
4. Mix together the chopped almonds and pine nuts, the vanilla seeds, flour, sugar, orange zest, baking powder and salt on a clean surface.
5. Make a well in the centre and crack in the eggs.
6. Work everything into a dough and shape it into two long rolls.
7. Bake on a baking sheet lined with greaseproof paper in the centre of the oven for about 25 minutes. Cut through one of the rolls to make sure they are completely done.
8. Reduce the temperature to 120°C/250°F/gas ½.
9. Cut the rolls at an angle into 1 cm (½ in) slices. Return the slices to the baking sheet.
10. Leave to dry in the centre of the oven for about 25 minutes or until completely dry.

chocolate biscotti with olives

I came up with the idea for this recipe while I was wondering whether chocolate and olives would mix. Adding pine nuts gave the biscuits a brilliant extra tweak!

MAKES 25 BISCUITS

1 organic egg
135 g (4 ¾ oz) caster sugar
210 g (7 ½ oz) plain flour
25 g (1 oz) good quality cocoa powder
1 teaspoon baking powder
½ teaspoon flaked salt
65 g (2 ½ oz) pitted black olives
50 g (2 oz) pine nuts
100 g (4 oz) good quality dark chocolate
   (70% cocoa solids)
50 ml (2 fl oz) olive oil
2 tablespoons cold water

1. Preheat the oven to 150°C/300°F/gas 2.
2. Beat together the egg and the sugar until pale and fluffy.
3. Mix together the flour, cocoa powder, baking powder and salt and blend into the egg mixture.
4. Chop the olives, pine nuts and chocolate coarsely and stir into the egg mixture.
5. Add the olive oil and water and work into a sticky dough.
6. Shape the dough into long rolls and put them on a baking sheet lined with greaseproof paper.
7. Bake in the centre of the oven for about 25 minutes. Take the rolls out and reduce the temperature to 120°C/250°F/gas ½.
8. Cut the rolls into 1 cm (½ in) slices. Return the slices to the baking sheet and leave to dry in the centre of the oven for about 20 minutes.

cardamom biscotti

MAKES 35 BISCUITS

1 teaspoon cardamom pods
1 vanilla pod
100 g (4 oz) unsalted butter, softened
90 g (3 ½ oz) caster sugar
45 g (1 ⅔ oz) demerara sugar
2 organic eggs
60 g (2 ⅓ oz) almonds
1 dried bitter almond
300 g (11 oz) plain flour
1 ½ teaspoons baking powder

1. Preheat the oven to 175°C/350°F/gas 4.
2. Pound the cardamom pods in a mortar. Split the vanilla pod lengthways and scrape out the seeds.
3. Beat together the butter, caster sugar, demerara sugar, vanilla seeds and cardamom until creamy.
4. Stir in one egg at a time.
5. Chop the almonds coarsely and grate the bitter almond.
6. Mix the almonds and the bitter almond with the flour and baking powder. Fold into the mixture.
7. Shape the dough into two long rolls and put them on a baking sheet lined with greaseproof paper.
8. Bake in the centre of the oven for about 25 minutes. Take the rolls out and reduce the temperature to 120°C/250°F/gas ½.
9. Cut the rolls into 1 cm (½ in) slices and return the slices to the oven.
10. Leave to dry in the centre of the oven for about 10 minutes or until completely dry.

almond butter biscuits

We served these classic cookies at one of my first jobs. They are really simple to make and are perfect both for a coffee break and as an accompaniment to a dessert. We used to serve them together with rhubarb soup and crème brûlée.

MAKES 60 COOKIES
200 g (7 oz) unsalted butter, softened
225 g (8 oz) caster sugar
zest of 1 lemon
200 g (7 oz) plain flour
3 organic eggs
100 g (4 oz) slivered almonds

1. Preheat the oven to 175°C/350°F/gas 4.
2. Beat the butter, the sugar and the lemon zest until creamy.
3. Carefully fold the flour into the mixture and finally stir in one egg at a time.
4. Pipe the mixture into 8–10 cm (3–4 in) long strings on a baking sheet lined with greaseproof paper. Space them well apart.
5. Decorate the mixture with slivered almonds and bake in the centre of the oven for 4–6 minutes or until golden.

grandma's brittle biscuits

My grandmother absolutely loves biscuits with her coffee. This is a very good, basic recipe that can be used for several different kinds of biscuit.

MAKES 50 BISCUITS
BASIC RECIPE
200 g (7 oz) unsalted butter, softened
1 teaspoon vanilla sugar
90 g (3 ½ oz) caster sugar
270–300 g (10–11 oz) plain flour

1. Preheat the oven to 175°C/350°F/gas 4.
2. Beat together the butter, the vanilla sugar and the caster sugar until pale and fluffy.
3. Add the flour and work into a dough but don't knead.
4. Put the dough in a plastic bag and leave to rest in the refrigerator for at least 1 hour.
5. Pick a flavouring of your choice (see the variations on page 22).

chocolate & hazelnut biscuits

MAKES 50 BISCUITS

1 batch of biscuit dough, see basic
    recipe page 21
100 g (4 oz) good quality dark chocolate
    (70% cocoa solids)
150 g (5 oz) hazelnuts

1. Prepare the biscuit dough according to the basic recipe.
2. Preheat the oven to 175°C/350°F/gas 4.
3. Chop the chocolate and the hazelnuts coarsely and knead them into the dough, reserving some hazelnuts for decoration.
4. Roll the dough into small balls and flatten them on a baking sheet lined with greaseproof paper. Put one hazelnut on each biscuit.
5. Bake in the centre of the oven for about 10 minutes or until lightly golden.

orange & pine nut biscuits

MAKES 50 BISCUITS

1 batch of biscuit dough, see basic
    recipe page 21
zest of 2 oranges
75 g (3 oz) pine nuts

1. Prepare the biscuit dough according to the basic recipe.
2. Preheat the oven to 175°C/350°F/gas 4.
3. Knead the orange zest and the pine nuts into the dough, reserving some pine nuts for decoration.
4. Roll the dough into small balls and flatten them on a baking sheet lined with greaseproof paper. Put one pine nut on each biscuit.
5. Bake in the centre of the oven for about 10 minutes or until lightly golden.

raspberry biscuits

MAKES 50 BISCUITS

1 batch of biscuit dough, see basic
    recipe page 21
100 ml (3 ½ fl oz) raspberry jam

1. Prepare the biscuit dough according to the basic recipe.
2. Preheat the oven to 175°C/350°F/gas 4.
3. Roll the dough into small balls and flatten them on a baking sheet lined with greaseproof paper.
4. Use your finger to make a small well in the centre of each biscuit. Place a small amount of jam in each depression.
5. Bake in the centre of the oven for about 10 minutes or until lightly golden.

cinnamon biscuits

MAKES 50 BISCUITS

1 batch of biscuit dough, see basic
    recipe page 21
4 tablespoons caster sugar
2 teaspoons ground cinnamon
egg for brushing

1. Prepare the biscuit dough according to the basic recipe.
2. Preheat the oven to 175°C/350°F/gas 4.
3. Mix the sugar and the cinnamon.
4. Roll the dough into small balls and flatten them on a baking sheet lined with greaseproof paper.
5. Score across each biscuit with a fork
6. Brush the biscuits with beaten egg and sprinkle the sugar and cinnamon on top.
7. Bake in the centre of the oven for about 10 minutes or until lightly golden.

lovely toffee slices

This wicked recipe for wonderful, chewy toffee slices is a contribution from my little sister Petronella. They are awesome!

MAKES 25 SLICES

100 g (4 oz) unsalted butter, softened

90 g (3 ½ oz) caster sugar

2 tablespoons golden syrup

135 g (4 ¾ oz) plain flour

½ teaspoon bicarbonate of soda

1 teaspoon vanilla sugar

1 teaspoon ground ginger

1. Preheat the oven to 175°C/350°F/gas 4.
2. Beat together the butter, caster sugar and syrup until creamy.
3. Mix the flour, bicarbonate of soda, vanilla sugar and ginger and blend into the mixture.
4. Shape the dough into two long rolls.
5. Put the rolls on a baking sheet lined with greaseproof paper and flatten them slightly. Score each biscuit with a fork.
6. Bake in the centre of the oven for 12–15 minutes or until golden.
7. Let the rolls cool a bit before cutting them diagonally. Leave the toffee slices to cool completely on the baking sheet.

hazelnut pyramids

When I bake hazelnut pyramids I sometimes add some crushed coffee beans, or flavour the mixture with frangelico (hazelnut liqueur). For that finishing touch I sometimes dip the bases in melted chocolate when the cakes have cooled. But they are lovely just the way they are too! Remember that the smaller the pyramids, the shorter the time they need in the oven.

MAKES 16 PYRAMIDS

50 g (2 oz) unsalted butter

200 g (7 oz) hazelnuts

90 g (3 ½ oz) caster sugar

1 organic egg

hazelnuts for decoration

1. Preheat the oven to 175°C/350°F/gas 4.
2. Melt the butter.
3. Process the hazelnuts in a blender to make a fine powder.
4. Mix the nuts with the butter, sugar and egg.
5. Use your fingers to shape the mixture into pyramids on a baking sheet lined with greaseproof paper. Put one hazelnut on to the top of each one.
6. Bake in the centre of the oven for about 18 minutes or until golden. Leave them to cool completely on the baking sheet.

lavender dream biscuits

I invented these happy dreams on a rainy day in the countryside when I thought I wasn't using enough lavender in my cooking. You can also try making your own lavender sugar, it's really easy! Blend fresh lavender flowers with caster sugar in a jar. After about a week the sugar will have absorbed the flavour. Superb for sprinkling on top of strawberries and vanilla ice cream.

MAKES 20 BISCUITS

100 g (4 oz) unsalted butter, softened
90 g (3 ½ oz) caster sugar
1 teaspoon vanilla sugar
150 g (5 oz) plain flour
½ teaspoon baking powder
1 tablespoon fresh or dried lavender
   flowers

1. Preheat the oven to 150°C/300°F/gas 2.
2. Beat the butter and the sugar until pale and creamy.
3. Mix the dry ingredients with the lavender flowers and stir into the butter cream to make a crumbly dough.
4. Shape small balls and put them on a baking sheet lined with greaseproof paper.
5. Bake in the centre of the oven for 15–20 minutes.

oatmeal biscuits

These crisp, wafer-thin biscuits are a Swedish classic. I love eating them together with strawberries and ice cream in the summer. The recipe is perfect if you're cooking in an unfamiliar kitchen because it's so easy. Just mix the ingredients and pop the biscuits in the oven. For a deluxe variation, dip half of each biscuit in melted chocolate.

MAKES 40 BISCUITS

150 g (5 oz) unsalted butter
80 g (3 ⅓ oz) rolled oats
180 g (6 ¼ oz) caster sugar
50 ml (2 fl oz) whipping cream
50 ml (2 fl oz) golden syrup
120 g (4 ½ oz) plain flour
½ teaspoon baking powder

1. Preheat the oven to 200°C/400°F/gas 6.
2. Melt the butter and mix with the rolled oats, sugar, whipping cream and syrup in a bowl.
3. Mix the flour with the baking powder and fold into the mixture.
4. Use two teaspoons to drop the mixture onto a baking sheet lined with greaseproof paper. Leave about 10 cm (4 in) between the biscuits because they will spread.
5. Bake in the centre of the oven for about 4 minutes or until golden.

on the cake plate

No garden party is complete without a good selection of splendid cakes. I am an absolute cake addict and adore these magnificent creations. In the following pages you'll find many of my favourite recipes for cherished classics, together with some inspiration from overseas, such as the New York-style Blueberry Cheesecake, Torta Della Nonna and Plum Clafouti. I have tried out many variations over the years, and so I'm happy to share with you the recipes that I think are a cut above the rest. You have my word they will not disappoint your guests whether they are popping round for coffee or are devouring your creations at that indulgent garden party.

nine juicy sponges

The trick to a spongy success is to beat the eggs and sugar until they are really fluffy. Never beat the flour into the mixture because that might give the sponge a rubber-like consistency. Instead, carefully fold the flour into the mixture. The basic recipe can be varied with all kinds of delicious flavourings (see below and page 34-35).

MAKES 1 CAKE
BASIC RECIPE
3 organic eggs
225 g (8 oz) caster sugar
1 teaspoon vanilla sugar
50 g (2 oz) unsalted butter
100 ml (3 ½ fl oz) milk
210 g (7 ½ oz) plain flour
2 teaspoons baking powder
1 pinch of salt
butter and dried breadcrumbs for the tin

1. Preheat the oven to 175°C/350°F/gas 4.
2. Beat together the eggs, caster sugar and vanilla sugar until white and fluffy.
3. Melt the butter and stir in milk. Mix into the egg mixture.
4. Mix the flour, baking powder and salt. Carefully fold into the egg mixture.
5. Choose a flavour (see variations) or just pour the mixture into a buttered ring mould coated with breadcrumbs.
6. Bake in the centre of the oven for 25–30 minutes or until a skewer inserted into the centre comes out clean.
7. Leave the sponge to cool slightly in the tin and then turn it out on to a plate or a wire rack.

old-style apple sponge

MAKES 1 CAKE
1 batch of sponge mixture, see basic
   recipe above
100 g (4 oz) homemade almond paste,
   see page 208
butter and dried breadcrumbs for the tin

FILLING
2 large cooking apples
30 g (1 ¼ oz) unsalted butter
2 tablespoons caster sugar
2 teaspoons ground cinnamon

1. Prepare the mixture according to the basic recipe and add the almond paste.
2. Core the apples and cut them into pieces. Fry the apples with the butter, sugar and cinnamon until they start browning and soften.
3. Butter a ring mould and coat it with breadcrumbs. Mix the apples with the cake mixture and pour it into the mould.
4. Bake in the centre of the preheated oven for 25–30 minutes or until a skewer inserted into the centre comes out clean.
5. Leave the sponge to cool slightly in the tin and then turn it out on to a plate or a wire rack.

on the cake plate

blackcurrant sponge

MAKES 1 CAKE

1 batch of sponge mixture, see basic
    recipe page 30
100 ml (3 ½ fl oz) buttermilk
zest and juice of 1 lemon
butter and dried breadcrumbs for the tin

FILLING

110 g (4 ¼ oz) fresh or frozen
    blackcurrants
1 tablespoon plain flour

1. Prepare the mixture according to the basic recipe but replace the milk with buttermilk.
2. Mix the lemon zest and juice into the mixture.
3. Toss the blackcurrants in the flour. Shake off excess flour and add the currants and the mixture in layers to a buttered ring mould coated with breadcrumbs.
4. Bake in the centre of the preheated oven for 25–30 minutes or until a skewer inserted into the centre comes out clean.
5. Leave the sponge to cool in the tin and then turn it out on to a plate or a wire rack.

cardamom sponge

MAKES 1 CAKE

1 batch of sponge mixture, see basic
    recipe page 30
1 tablespoon cardamom pods
butter and dried breadcrumbs for the tin
icing sugar

1. Prepare the mixture according to the basic recipe but add finely ground cardamom seeds to the milk and bring the milk to the boil before stirring it into the butter.
2. Pour into a buttered ring mould coated with breadcrumbs.
3. Bake in the centre of the preheated oven for 25–30 minutes or until a skewer inserted into the centre comes out clean.
4. Leave the sponge to cool in the tin and then turn it out on to a plate or a wire rack. Dust with icing sugar before serving.

amazing saffron sponge

MAKES 1 CAKE

1 batch of sponge mixture, see basic
    recipe page 30
1 pinch of saffron
1 tablespoon light rum
butter and desiccated coconut for the tin

1. Prepare the mixture according to the basic recipe but add the saffron to the milk and bring the milk to the boil before stirring it into the butter. Flavour the mixture with the rum.
2. Pour into a buttered ring mould coated with desiccated coconut.
3. Bake in the centre of the preheated oven for 25–30 minutes or until a skewer inserted into the centre comes out clean.
4. Leave the sponge to cool in the tin and then turn it out on to a plate or a wire rack.

soft gingerbread sponge

MAKES 1 CAKE

1 batch of sponge mixture,
    see basic recipe page 30
100 ml (3 ½ fl oz) buttermilk
1 teaspoon ground ginger
2 teaspoons ground cinnamon
2 teaspoons ground clove
zest of 1 orange
butter and slivered almonds for the tin

1. Prepare the mixture according to the basic recipe but replace the milk with buttermilk. Add the spices and orange zest.
2. Pour into a buttered ring mould coated with slivered almonds.
3. Bake in the centre of the preheated oven for 25–30 minutes or until a skewer inserted into the centre comes out clean.
4. Leave the sponge to cool in the tin and then turn it out on to a plate or a wire rack.

lemon poppy seed sponge

MAKES 1 CAKE

1 batch of sponge mixture, see basic
    recipe page 30
zest of 3 lemons
juice of 1 lemon
30 g (1 ¼ oz) poppy seeds

LEMON ICING

350 g (11 ½ oz) icing sugar
75 ml (3 fl oz) freshly squeezed lemon
    juice
butter and dried breadcrumbs for the tin

1. Prepare the mixture according to the basic recipe and add the
   lemon zest and juice and the poppy seeds.
2. Pour into a buttered ring mould coated with breadcrumbs.
3. Bake in the centre of the preheated oven for 25–30 minutes or
   until a skewer inserted into the centre comes out clean.
4. Leave the sponge to cool in the tin and then turn it out on to
   a plate or a wire rack.
5. Mix together the icing sugar and lemon juice until smooth
   then drizzle the icing over the sponge.

coconut tosca sponge

MAKES 1 CAKE

1 batch of sponge mixture, see basic
    recipe page 30
butter and dried breadcrumbs for the tin

CRUNCHY TOP

25 g (1 oz) butter
50 ml (2 fl oz) light syrup
75 ml (3 fl oz) single cream
90 g (3 ½ oz) desiccated coconut
90 g (3 ½ oz) caster sugar

1. Prepare the mixture according to the basic recipe. Butter a
   23 cm (9 inch) springform cake tin and coat with breadcrumbs.
2. Pour in the mixture. Bake in the centre of the preheated oven
   for about 25 minutes.
3. In the meantime, prepare the crunchy top. Stir together the
   ingredients for the topping in a saucepan. Bring to the boil and
   boil for about 5 minutes.
4. Remove the cake from the oven and cover the sponge with the
   crunchy top. Return the cake to the oven and bake for another
   15 minutes or until the topping is golden.
5. Leave the sponge to cool before removing the sides of the
   springform cake tin.

strawberry & rhubarb sponge

MAKES 1 CAKE

zest of 2 limes
juice of 1 lime
butter and dried breadcrumbs for the tin

FILLING

90 g (3 ½) oz fresh strawberries
1 large rhubarb stick
30 g (1 ¼ oz) icing sugar
1 tablespoon plain flour

1. Prepare the mixture according to the basic recipe. Add the lime
   zest and juice to the mixture.
2. Cut the strawberries and the rhubarb into thin slices and blend
   them with the icing sugar and flour. Add to the cake mixture.
3. Pour the mixture into a buttered ring mould coated with
   breadcrumbs.
4. Bake in the centre of the preheated oven for 25–30 minutes or
   until a skewer inserted into the centre comes out clean.
5. Leave the sponge to cool in the tin and then turn it out on to a
   plate or a wire rack.

chocolate chip walnut brownies

A brownie should have a moist and creamy texture. I learned this recipe when I worked at a French patisserie in Stockholm. Serve it either as a coffee break treat or as a dessert together with softened vanilla ice cream.

MAKES 12 BROWNIES

350 g (12 oz) unsalted butter, softened
550 g (1 lb/2 oz) caster sugar
150 g (5 oz) good quality cocoa powder
100 ml (3 ½ fl oz) golden syrup
6 organic eggs, beaten
180 g (6 ¼ oz) plain flour
400 g (14 oz) good quality white
    chocolate
250 g (9 oz) walnuts
walnuts for decoration

FUDGE GLAZE

300 ml (½ pint) whipping cream
100 ml (3 ½ fl oz) milk
100 ml (3 ½ fl oz) golden syrup
1 teaspoon ground ginger
400 g (14 oz) good quality dark chocolate
    (70% cocoa solids)

1. Preheat the oven to 175°C/350°F/gas 4.
2. Mix the butter and the sugar until pale and creamy.
3. Stir in the cocoa powder and syrup.
4. Mix in the eggs one at a time and then carefully add the flour into the mixture.
5. Chop the chocolate coarsely and blend into the mixture together with the chopped walnuts.
6. Line a square cake tin, 30 x 30 cm (12 x 12 in) with greaseproof paper. Pour in the mixture.
7. Bake in the centre of the oven for 15–25 minutes or until a skewer inserted into the centre comes out slightly sticky.
8. Leave the cake to cool.
9. Bring the cream, milk, syrup and ginger to the boil. Take the saucepan off the heat.
10. Chop the chocolate finely and blend it into the warm mixture. Stir until the chocolate melts.
11. Spread the glaze over the cake and sprinkle over a few whole walnuts. Leave in the fridge until set. Cut the cake in squares.

plum clafouti

This French eggy pudding is best served at room temperature accompanied with softened vanilla ice cream and lightly whipped cream. The pudding is easy to vary with all kinds of fresh berries. Just sprinkle the berries into the mixture, without frying. The clafouti also tastes really good made with apples, pears or rhubarb. Cut these fruits into pieces or slices and fry them like the plums.

MAKES 1 CAKE

8 ripe plums

30 g (1 ¼ oz) unsalted butter

2 tablespoons caster sugar

1 teaspoon ground cinnamon

butter and caster sugar for the tin

slivered almonds to decorate

CLAFOUTI MIXTURE

50 g (2 oz) slivered almonds

½ vanilla pod

30 g (1 ¼ oz) plain flour

70 g (2 ⅔ oz) caster sugar

zest of 1 lime

250 ml (8 fl oz) whipping cream

2 organic eggs

2 organic egg yolks

1. Preheat the oven to 175°C/350°F/gas 4.
2. Halve and stone the plums. Fry them, cut side down in the butter, sugar and cinnamon. Leave to cool.
3. Make the clafouti. Grind the almonds in a blender to make a fine powder.
4. Split the vanilla pod lengthways and scrape out the seeds. Mix together the almond powder, flour, sugar and lime zest.
5. Add the cream, eggs, egg yolks and beat until smooth.
6. Butter a 2 litre (3 ½ pint) ovenproof dish and sprinkle with sugar. Pour in the mixture.
7. Arrange the plums, cut side up, in the dish and sprinkle over the slivered almonds.
8. Bake in the centre of the oven for 35–40 minutes or until golden and the mixture is set.

speedy berry cake

I have spent many summer days in the Stockholm archipelago, where some friends have a summer cottage. Summertime is berry cake time. Try this delicious quick and easy cake, which can be varied with all kinds of different berries.

MAKES 1 CAKE
120 g (4 ½ oz) butter
135 g (4 ¾ oz) caster sugar
120 g (4 ½ oz) plain flour
1 ½ teaspoons baking powder
1 pinch of salt
1 organic egg
90 g (3 ½ oz) fresh or frozen berries
1 tablespoon plain flour
butter and dried breadcrumbs for the tin

1. Preheat the oven to 175°C/350°F/gas 4.
2. Bring the butter and the sugar to the boil and simmer for 1 minute. Leave to cool.
3. Mix together the flour, baking powder and salt and fold into the butter mixture. Stir in the egg.
4. Pour the mixture into a buttered 23 cm (9 in) springform cake tin covered with breadcrumbs or a small ovenproof dish.
5. Toss the berries in the flour, shake off any excess and sprinkle the berries over the cake.
6. Bake in the centre of the oven for about 20 minutes or until golden.

pecan banana bread

This incredibly moist cake is a wonderful treat at a coffee break. It is delicious for dessert as well, especially if you toast the slices in a dry frying pan. Like toast with ice cream!

MAKES 1 CAKE

150 g (5 oz) unsalted butter, softened
90 g (3 ½ oz) caster sugar
120 g (4 ½ oz) icing sugar
4 ripe bananas
2 organic eggs
175 g (6 oz) plain flour
1 teaspoon baking powder
½ teaspoon ground cinnamon
½ teaspoon ground ginger
1 pinch of salt
75 g (3 oz) pecan nuts
butter and dried breadcrumbs for the tin

1. Preheat the oven to 175°C/350°F/gas 4.
2. Beat together the butter, caster sugar and icing sugar until pale and creamy.
3. Mash the bananas and stir them into the mixture. Beat in the eggs.
4. Mix the dry ingredients with the whole pecan nuts (reserving a few to sprinkle on top of the cake) and carefully blend into the mixture.
5. Pour the mixture into a buttered rectangular 1 kg (2 lb) cake tin covered with breadcrumbs and bake in the centre of the oven for about 30 minutes or until a skewer inserted into the centre comes out clean.

semolina cake with cherries

A friend of mine gave me the recipe for this crunchy and rather special cake. His mother bakes it, and he always tells me it is the best cake ever.

MAKES 1 CAKE

175 g (6 oz) caster sugar
2 organic eggs
150 g (5 oz) unsalted butter, softened
150 g (5 oz) plain flour
1 pinch of salt
75 g (3 oz) semolina
400 g (14 oz) fresh or canned cherries, pitted
butter and dried breadcrumbs for the tin

1. Preheat the oven to 200°C/400°F/gas 6.
2. Beat together the sugar and the eggs until pale and fluffy.
3. Mix in the butter.
4. Mix together the flour, salt and semolina and blend into the mixture.
5. Pour the mixture into a buttered 23 cm (9 in) springform cake tin covered with breadcrumbs. Lightly press the cherries into the mixture.
6. Bake in the centre of the oven for 25–30 minutes or until a skewer inserted into the centre comes out clean.

chocolate darlings

The best recipes are passed down from genenation to genenation and I've borrowed this one from my mum's recipe book. These moist and fluffy cakes are a Swedish classic.

MAKES 1 CAKE
5 organic eggs
350 g (11 ½ oz) caster sugar
275 g (9 oz) plain flour
3 teaspoons baking powder
1 pinch of salt
5 tablespoons good quality cocoa
   powder
200 ml (7 fl oz) water
300 g (11 oz) unsalted butter, melted
200 g (7 oz) plain chocolate
   (or good quality dark chocolate,
   70% cocoa solids)
90 g (3 ½ oz) desiccated coconut

CHOCOLATE ICING
200 ml (7 fl oz) whipping cream
2 tablespoons espresso coffee
200 g (7 oz) good quality dark chocolate,
   70% cocoa solids

1. Preheat the oven to 200°C/400°F/gas 6.
2. Beat together the eggs and the sugar until they are pale and fluffy.
3. Mix together the dry ingredients and carefully blend into the egg mixture.
4. Add the water and melted butter and stir to combine.
5. Like a 40 x 35 cm (16 x 4 in) cake tin with greaseproof paper. Pour the mixture into the tin.
6. Sprinkle coarsely chopped chocolate over the top.
7. Bake in the centre of the oven for 10–15 minutes or until a skewer inserted into the centre comes out slightly sticky. Leave to cool.
8. Bring the whipping cream to the boil, stir in the coffee and leave to cool slightly.
9. Finely chop the chocolate, add the cream and stir until melted. Spread the icing over the cake.
10. Sprinkle desiccated coconut on top and leave to set.
11. Cut into squares.

new york blueberry cheesecake

This is a wonderful original recipe from a diner in New York. I love this cake, and even my American friend says it's the best cheesecake ever. It's also very easy to make. The cake is easier to cut if you serve it chilled. If the cake gets stuck in the tin use a small knife to run round the edge to loosen it.

MAKES 1 CAKE

CRUST

300 g (11 oz) digestive biscuits
150 g (5 oz) unsalted butter, melted

FILLING

600 g (1 lb/5 oz) cream cheese
250 ml (8 fl oz) curd cheese
90 g (3 ½ oz) caster sugar
50 g (2 oz) cornflour
2 teaspoons vanilla sugar
3 organic eggs
100 ml (3 ½ fl oz) whipping cream
200 g (7 oz) good quality white chocolate
75 g (3 oz) fresh or frozen blueberries

1. Preheat the oven to 175°C/350°F/gas 4.
2. Grind the biscuits finely in a blender and mix the crumbs with the melted butter.
3. Press the imixture into the bottom of a nonstick 23 cm (9 in) springform cake tin.
4. Bake in the centre of the oven for about 10 minutes. Leave to cool.
5. Beat together the cream cheese and curd cheese until creamy.
6. Mix together the sugar, cornflour and vanilla sugar and add to the cheese mixture.
7. Beat in the eggs, one at a time, at a time and then fold in the whipping cream.
8. Break the chocolate into pieces and melt in a bowl set over a pan of simmering water. Stir the chocolate into the cheesecake filling.
9. Pour the filling over the crust and sprinkle the blueberries on top.
10. Bake in the centre of the oven for about 40 minutes. To prevent the cheesecake from browning, cover it with foil when it is golden brown.
11. Turn off the oven and leave the cheesecake to continue cooking in the residual heat for 30 minutes.

the best carrot cake ever

You can find an almost infinite number of variations of this moist American cake, but this is definitely the best one I have ever tried.

MAKES 1 CAKE

3 organic eggs

270 g (9 ½ oz) caster sugar

180 g (6 ¼ oz) plain flour

1 teaspoon vanilla sugar

3 teaspoons baking powder

1 ½ teaspoons ground cinnamon

1 teaspoon ground cardamom

½ teaspoon ground ginger

1 pinch of salt

150 ml (5 fl oz) sunflower oil

450 g (1 lb) grated carrots

butter and dried breadcrumbs for the tin

CREAM CHEESE LIME FROSTING

65 g (2 ½ oz) unsalted butter, softened

240 g (8 ½ oz) icing sugar

1 teaspoon vanilla sugar

zest of 1 lime

100 g (4 oz) cream cheese

1. Preheat the oven to 150°C/300°F/gas 2.
2. Beat together the eggs and the sugar until pale and fluffy.
3. Mix together all the dry ingredients and blend into the egg mixture.
4. Stir in the oil and carrots.
5. Pour the mixture into a buttered 23 cm (9 in) springform cake tin covered with breadcrumbs.
6. Bake in the centre of the oven for about 55 minutes or until a skewer inserted into the centre comes out clean.
7. Leave the cake to cool.
8. Mix together the ingredients for the frosting until creamy and smooth, then spread the frosting over the top of the cake.

torta della nonna

Torta della nonna means granny's cake, and it is an Italian cheesecake with almonds, egg and cream cheese. It's usually quite complicated to make, but I have made my own simple version. I like to serve it with lightly whipped cream.

MAKES 1 CAKE
150 g (5 oz) unsalted butter, softened
300 g (11 oz) homemade almond paste,
    see recipe page 208
6 organic eggs
250 g (9 oz) ricotta cheese
zest of 1 lemon
zest of 1 orange
1 teaspoon almond extract
25 g (1 oz) plain flour
butter and slivered almonds for the tin
pine nuts
icing sugar

1. Preheat the oven to 175°C/350°F/gas 4.
2. Mix together the butter and the grated almond paste until creamy.
3. Add the eggs, one at a time, beating to make a smooth mixture.
4. Stir in the cheese, citrus zest and almond extract. Fold in the flour.
5. Butter a 23 cm (9 in) springform cake tin and cover with crushed slivered almonds.
6. Pour in the mixture and sprinkle pine nuts over the top.
7. Bake in the centre of the oven for 25–30 minutes or until a skewer inserted into the centre comes out clean.
8. Dust icing sugar over the cake before serving.

sticky chocolate cake

Everyone's got their own favourite version of this simple, yet incredibly moreish, Swedish classic. I like mine both toffeelike and sticky, and here's my best recipe.

MAKES 1 CAKE
50 g (2 oz) unsalted butter
50 ml (2 fl oz) vegetable oil
2 organic eggs
180 g (6 ¼ oz) caster sugar
75 g (3 oz) brown sugar
150 g (5 oz) plain flour
4 tablespoons good quality cocoa powder
2 teaspoons baking powder
1 teaspoon vanilla sugar
1 pinch of salt
butter and dried breadcrumbs for the tin
50 g (2 oz) good quality dark chocolate
    (70% cocoa solids)

1. Preheat the oven to 150°C/300°F/gas 2.
2. Melt the butter in a saucepan. Add the oil.
3. Beat together the eggs, caster sugar and brown sugar until pale and fluffy. Stir in the hot butter.
4. Mix together the dry ingredients and blend into the mixture.
5. Butter a 23 cm (9 in) springform cake tin and cover it with breadcrumbs. Pour the mixture into the tin. Break the chocolate into pieces and add to the mixture.
6. Bake in the centre of the oven for about 30 minutes or until a skewer inserted into the centre comes out slightly sticky.

tarts, flans & pies

These recipes are some of my friends' big favourites, and they have a place in my heart too. Some are old classics and some are new ideas. If you are in a hurry, I can recommend The Apple Lady's Crumble, Easy-to-make French Fruit Flan or Strawberry Flan with Toffee Cream. If you like being well-prepared, take a look at the Royale Pies which are really practical because you can freeze them unbaked then stick them straight in the oven when your guests are on their way: not just really tasty but efficient too!

classic shortcrust pastry dough

When you make shortcrust pastry dough don't knead it too much or it will turn dense and lose its crustiness. You can easily make a chocolate shortcrust pastry dough by adding 2 tablespoons of cocoa powder.

MAKES ENOUGH FOR 2 TARTS
BASIC RECIPE
150 g (5 oz) cold unsalted butter, diced
240 g (8 ½ oz) plain flour
30 g (1 ¼ oz) icing sugar
1 organic egg
½ tablespoon cold water

1. Put the butter, flour and sugar in a bowl and mix with your fingertips to make breadcrumbs.
2. Add the egg and the water and gently work the dough to bind the ingredients together. Don't knead.
3. Cover with clingfilm and leave to rest in the refrigerator for 30 minutes.

classic crumble

This crumble mix can be kept in the refrigerator for a few days. Then all you have to do is take it out of the fridge when you want to sprinkle it over a pie.

MAKES ENOUGH FOR 1 PIE
BASIC RECIPE
100 g (4 oz) cold unsalted butter, diced
90 g (3 ½ oz) plain flour
70 g (2 ⅔ oz) caster sugar
25 g (1 oz) slivered almonds
60 g (2 ⅓ oz) rolled oats

1. Put the butter, flour and sugar in a bowl and mix with your fingertips to make breadcrumbs.
2. Mix the slivered almonds and rolled oats into the breadcrumbs.

oat pastry dough

Pies made with an oat pastry dough are really lovely! Don't bake them for too long because the pastry easily turns hard. It's ready when it starts to turn light brown.

MAKES ENOUGH FOR 1 PIE
BASIC RECIPE
175 g (6 oz) unsalted butter, softened
180 g (6 ¼ oz) plain flour
135 g (4 ¾ oz) caster sugar
65 g (2 ½ oz) rolled oats

1. Preheat the oven to 175°C/350°F/gas 4.
2. Melt the butter and stir in the flour, sugar and rolled oats.
3. Press the dough into a pie tin.
4. Bake blind in the centre of the oven for about 15 minutes.

french royale in nine ways

This pie is both super tasty and really practical because you can make it complete with crust and filling and freeze it uncooked. Then all you have to do is take the pie out of the freezer and put it in the oven. It's a perfect surprise when friends come over unexpectedly or to serve as a dessert if you want to prepare it in advance for a party.

MAKES 1 PIE/SERVES 8
BASIC RECIPE
1 batch of classic shortcrust pastry
    dough, see basic recipe page 55

ROYALE MIXTURE
100 g (4 oz) homemade almond paste,
    see recipe page 208
3 organic eggs
200 ml (7 fl oz) curd cheese
100 ml (3 ½ fl oz) crème fraiche
90 g (3 ½ oz) caster sugar
filling (see variations)

1. Prepare the shortcrust pastry according to the basic recipe.
2. Preheat the oven to 175°C/350°F/gas 4.
3. Roll out the dough and use it to line a loose-bottomed tin.
4. Grate the almond paste and mix it with the other ingredients for the royale mixture.
5. Flavour with a filling of your choice (see below) and bake for 30-40 minutes in the oven.

berry royale

MAKES 1 PIE/SERVES 8
1 prepared French royale with mixture,
    see basic recipe above
150 g (5 oz) mixed fresh berries
    (or frozen)
1 handful of slivered almonds

1. Spread the berries on top of the pie and sprinkle with the slivered almonds.
2. Bake in the lower part of the preheated oven for 30–40 minutes or until golden and the mixture is set (or put the prepared pie in the freezer and bake it on another occasion).

fig royale

MAKES 1 PIE/SERVES 8
1 prepared French royale with mixture,
    see basic recipe above
8 ripe figs
30 g (1 ¼ oz) unsalted butter
2 tablespoons caster sugar
2 teaspoons ground cinnamon
1 handful of slivered almonds

1. Split the figs in half and cut off the stems. Fry, cut side down, in a pan with the butter, sugar and cinnamon for about 3 minutes.
2. Spread the figs over the pie with cut side up. Sprinkle with the slivered almonds.
3. Bake in the lower part of the preheated oven for 30–40 minutes or until golden and the mixture is set (or put the prepared pie in the freezer and bake it on another occasion).

tarts, flans & pies

blackberry & lemon royale

MAKES 1 PIE/SERVES 8

1 prepared French royale with mixture,
  see basic recipe page 56
zest of 2 lemons
150 g (5 oz) fresh or frozen blackberries
1 handful of slivered almonds

1. Spread the lemon zest and blackberries over the pie. Sprinkle with the slivered almonds.
2. Bake in the lower part of the preheated oven for 30–40 minutes or until golden and the mixture is set (or put the prepared pie in the freezer and bake it on another occasion).

nectarine royale

MAKES 1 PIE/SERVES 8

1 prepared French royale with mixture,
  see basic recipe page 56
4 ripe nectarines
1 handful of slivered almonds

1. Halve the nectarines and remove the stones. Cut the flesh into thin slices.
2. Arrange the nectarines over the pie. Sprinkle with the slivered almonds.
3. Bake in the lower part of the preheated oven for 30–40 minutes or until golden and the mixture is set (or put the prepared pie in the freezer and bake it on another occasion).

redcurrant royale

MAKES 1 PIE/SERVES 8

1 prepared French royale with mixture,
  see basic recipe page 56
150 g (5 oz) fresh or frozen redcurrants
1 handful of slivered almonds

1. Spread the redcurrants over the pie. Sprinkle with the slivered almonds.
2. Bake in the lower part of the preheated oven for 30–40 minutes or until golden and the mixture is set (or put the prepared pie in the freezer and bake it on another occasion).

plum royale

MAKES 1 PIE/SERVES 8

1 prepared French royale with mixture,
  see basic recipe page 56
6 ripe plums
30 g (1 ¼ oz) unsalted butter
2 tablespoons caster sugar
2 teaspoons ground cinnamon
1 handful of slivered almonds

1. Halve the plums and remove the stones.
2. Melt the butter, sugar and cinnamon in a frying pan and cook the plums, cut side down for about 3 minutes.
3. Spread the plums, cut side up, over the pie. Sprinkle with the slivered almonds.
4. Bake in the lower part of the preheated oven for 30–40 minutes or until golden and the mixture is set (or put the prepared pie in the freezer and bake it on another occasion).

apricot royale

MAKES 1 PIE/SERVES 8

1 prepared French royale with mixture,
    see basic recipe page 56
8 ripe apricots
30 g (1 ¼ oz) unsalted butter
2 tablespoons caster sugar
2 teaspoons ground cinnamon
1 teaspoon cardamom pods
1 handful of slivered almonds

1. Halve the apricots and remove the stones.
2. Melt the butter, sugar, cinnamon and ground cardamom in a frying pan and cook the apricots, cut side down, for about 3 minutes.
3. Spread the apricots, cut side up, over the pie. Sprinkle with the slivered almonds.
4. Bake in the lower part of the preheated oven for 30–40 minutes or until golden and the mixture is set (or put the prepared pie in the freezer and bake it on another occasion).

pear royale

MAKES 1 PIE/SERVES 8

1 prepared French royale with mixture,
    see basic recipe page 56
8 canned pear halves
1 handful of slivered almonds

1. Drain the pears and put them, cut side down, on a chopping-board. Slice the halves lengthways and press down gently to spread them like a fan.
2. Arrange the fans, cut side down, over the pie. Sprinkle with the slivered almonds.
3. Bake in the lower part of the preheated oven for 30–40 minutes or until golden and the mixture is set (or put the prepared pie in the freezer and bake it on another occasion).

raspberry royale with lime

MAKES 1 PIE/SERVES 8

1 prepared French royale with mixture,
    see basic recipe page 56
zest of 2 limes
150 g (5 oz) fresh or frozen raspberries
1 handful of slivered almonds

1. Spread the lime zest and raspberries over the pie. Sprinkle with the slivered almonds.
2. Bake in the lower part of the preheated oven for 30–40 minutes or until golden and the mixture is set (or put the prepared pie in the freezer and bake it on another occasion).

nutty fig tart

This recipe is a contribution from an Italian friend. The pie is irresistibly nutty, and I like to serve it with softened vanilla ice cream or lightly whipped cream. When you are buying chocolate keep an eye on the cocoa content. I like to use chocolate containing 70% cocoa solids when baking. The high cocoa content gives a rich taste but without the bitterness that chocolate exceeding 70% sometimes has. I never use cooking chocolate because the quality is too low, and it also contains a lot of unnecessary additives.

MAKES 1 PIE/SERVES 10

**1 batch of classic shortcrust pastry
   dough, see basic recipe page 55**

FILLING
350 g (12 oz) almonds
300 g (11 oz) unsalted butter, softened
225 g (8 oz) caster sugar
3 organic eggs
zest of 1 orange
65 g (2 ½ oz) plain flour
150 g (5 oz) good quality dark chocolate
   (70% cocoa solids)
8–10 fresh figs

1. Prepare the shortcrust pastry according to the basic recipe. Roll out the dough and use it to line a loose-bottomed pie tin.
2. Preheat the oven to 175°C/350°F/gas 4.
3. Blanch the almonds and grind in a blender to make a fine powder.
4. Beat the butter and the sugar until pale and creamy.
5. Stir in the orange zest. Add the eggs one at a time. beating the mixture after each addition.
6. Carefully blend the almond powder and flour into the egg mixture. Add the coarsely chopped chocolate.
7. Pour the mixture into the tin.
8. Cut a cross in the tops of some of the figs and open them out slightly to reveal the seeds. Cut the remaining figs into pieces. Add all the figs to the mixture.
9. Bake in the lower part of the oven for about 55 minutes or until golden and the mixture is set.

american apple pie

Shortcrust pastry dough should be handled as little as possible. All the ingredients should be cold and just about hold together to form a dough. You can make the dough in advance and keep it in the freezer or line the tin with the pastry and freeze the whole thing, which makes it easier when you have a sudden urge to make a pie. There are several ways to avoid the edges from sliding down when you prebake the pastry shell. I usually prop them up with tin foil, but just make sure that the foil is stuck on hard enough. You can also fill the pastry shell with dried beans. For this recipe you don't need to prebake the pastry.

MAKES 1 PIE/SERVES 8

1 batch of classic shortcrust pastry
    dough, see basic recipe page 55
egg and milk for brushing
demerara sugar

FILLING

12 big Granny Smith apples
juice of 1 lemon
50 g (2 oz) butter
4 tablespoons caster sugar
2 teaspoons ground cinnamon
1 teaspoon ground ginger

1. Prepare the shortcrust pastry according to the basic recipe.
2. Preheat the oven to 175°C/350°F/gas 4.
3. Core and slice the apples and put them in a bowl with the lemon juice.
4. Melt the butter in a frying pan. Add the sugar, cinnamon and ginger and fry the apples. You will find it easier to do this in two batches. Transfer the apples to a plate to cool.
5. Divide the dough into two pieces, one a bit bigger than the other.
6. Put the larger piece of dough on a lightly floured surface and roll it out to a circle about 30 cm (12 in) across.
7. Supporting the pastry on your rolling pin, use it to line a 23 cm (9 in) loose-bottomed pie tin. Press the pastry gently against the bottom and sides of the tin, leaving the excess hanging over the edge.
8. Fill the pastry case with the fried apples.
9. Roll out the smaller piece of pastry to a circle about 25 cm (10 in) across.
10. Beat an egg with a splash of milk and brush the edges of the pastry. Put the top crust on top of the pie.
11. Pinch the pastry discs firmly together and trim away excess pastry hanging over the sides.
12. Put the pie tin on a baking sheet, brush the top with the egg mixture and sprinkle over demerara sugar. Make slits (to make sunbeams) or pinch small holes in the top crust. Bake in the lower part of the oven for about 35 minutes or until golden.

the apple lady's crumble

When I was young we used to steal apples from the Apple Lady. I named this tasty crumble pie after her. Serve the pie with lightly whipped cream or speedy vanilla custard (see page 208).

MAKES 1 BIG PIE/4 SMALL PIES
BASIC RECIPE
250 g (9 oz) cold unsalted butter, diced
135 g (4 ¾ oz) demerara sugar
65 g (2 ½ oz) desiccated coconut
150 g (5 oz) plain flour
60 g (2 ¼ oz) rolled oats

1. Put the butter in a bowl. Add the sugar, coconut and flour and mix lightly with your fingertips to make breadcrumbs.
2. Carefully blend in the rolled oats without breaking them.
3. Add the filling of your choice (see below), then bake for about 25 minutes.

blueberry crumble

MAKES 1 BIG PIE/4 SMALL PIES
1 batch of Apple Lady's Crumble, see basic recipe above
butter for the dish and to dot on top of the pie

FILLING
675 g (1 ½ lb) fresh or frozen blueberries
zest of 2 lemons
90 g (3 ½ oz) caster sugar
2 tablespoons cornflour

1. Prepare the crumble according to the basic recipe.
2. Preheat the oven to 200°C/400°F/gas 6.
3. Mix the blueberries, lemon zest, sugar and cornflour in a bowl.
4. Cover the bottom of a buttered ovenproof dish with the berries. Spread the crumble over the top and dot with some butter.
5. Bake in the centre of the preheated oven for about 25 minutes or until golden.

cherry crumble

MAKES 1 BIG PIE/4 SMALL PIES
1 batch of Apple Lady's Crumble, see basic recipe above
butter for the dish and to dot on top of the pie

FILLING
675 g (1 ½ lb) fresh cherries
zest of 1 orange
75 g (3 oz) dark muscovado sugar
2 tablespoons cornflour

1. Prepare the crumble according to the basic recipe.
2. Preheat the oven to 200°C/400°F/gas 6.
3. Pit the cherries and mix them with the orange zest, sugar and cornflour in a bowl.
4. Cover the bottom of a buttered ovenproof dish with the cherries. Spread the crumble over the top and dot with some butter.
5. Bake in the centre of the preheated oven for about 25 minutes or until golden.

strawberry & rhubarb crumble

MAKES 1 BIG PIE/4 SMALL PIES

1 batch of crumble, see basic recipe
    page 69
butter for the dish and to dot on top of
    the pie

FILLING

3 large rhubarb sticks
270 g (9 ½ oz) fresh strawberries
4 pieces of crystallised ginger
90 g (3 ½ oz) caster sugar
2 tablespoons cornflour

1. Prepare the crumble according to the basic recipe.
2. Preheat the oven to 200°C/400°F/gas 6.
3. Wash and chop the rhubarb, removing any stringy bits. Hull and halve the strawberries.
4. Finely chop the ginger and mix it with the rhubarb, strawberries, sugar and cornflour.
5. Cover the bottom of a buttered ovenproof dish with the fruit. Spread the crumble over the top and dot with butter.
6. Bake in the centre of the preheated oven for about 25 minutes or until golden.

peach & apple crumble

MAKES 1 BIG PIE/4 SMALL PIES

1 batch of crumble, see basic recipe
    page 69
butter for the dish and to dot on top of
    the pie

FILLING

4 ripe cooking apples
4 ripe nectarines
30 g (1 ¼ oz) unsalted butter
2 tablespoons caster sugar
2 teaspoons ground cinnamon
2 teaspoons ground ginger

1. Prepare the crumble according to the basic recipe.
2. Preheat the oven to 200°C/400°F/gas 6.
3. Cut the fruit into pieces and fry (in batches if necessary) in the butter, sugar and spices.
4. Cover the bottom of a buttered ovenproof dish with the fruit. Spread the crumble over the top and dot with butter.
5. Bake in the centre of the preheated oven for about 25 minutes or until golden.

my garden crumble

MAKES 1 BIG PIE/4 SMALL PIES

1 batch of crumble, see basic recipe
    page 69
butter for the dish and to dot on top of
    the pie

FILLING

540 g (1 ¼ lb) mixed fresh garden berries
90 g (3 ½ oz) caster sugar
1 tablespoon cornflour

1. Prepare the crumble according to the basic recipe.
2. Preheat the oven to 200°C/400°F/gas 6.
3. Mix the berries with the sugar and cornflour in a bowl.
4. Cover the bottom of a buttered ovenproof dish with the berries. Spread the crumble over the top and dot with butter.
5. Bake in the centre of the preheated oven for about 25 minutes or until golden.

crunchy blueberry pie

Nothing can compare with my granny's wonderful blueberry pie. I just love this recipe!

MAKES 1 PIE/SERVES 8

1 batch of classic shortcrust pastry
    dough or oat pastry dough,
    see recipe page 55

FILLING

250 g (9 oz) fresh or frozen blueberries
200 ml (7 fl oz) blueberry jam
1 tablespoon balsamic vinegar
2 ½ tablespoons cornflour

CRUNCHY TOPPING

75 g (3 oz) unsalted butter
100 g (4 oz) rolled oats
135 g (4 ¾ oz) caster sugar

1. Prepare the pastry according to the basic recipe.
2. Preheat the oven to 175°C/350°F/gas 4.
3. Roll out the pastry on a lightly floured board to a circle and use it to line a loose-bottomed flan tin. Prick the base with a fork. Fill the case with foil or beans and bake blind in the oven for about 10 minutes.
4. Make the filling by mixing together the blueberries, jam and vinegar. Stir in the cornflour and pour the mixture into the pastry case.
5. Make the topping by melting the butter. Stir in the oats and sugar and leave to stand for 2-3 minutes.
6. Sprinkle the topping over the filling and bake in the centre of the oven for about 25 minutes or until golden.

butterscotch pecan pie

This pie is good all year round, summer as well as at Christmas! If you'd like to vary the flavouring you can add some ginger or cardamom. To check if the butterscotch is ready, drop a little of the mixture into a glass of really cold water. If it hardens a little so that you can form a soft, little ball it is ready and will set in the pie. I allow the pie to come to room temperature before serving, because keeping it in the fridge makes the filling a bit hard. Serve the pie accompanied by Raspberry Fool Cream (see page 211).

MAKES 1 PIE/SERVES 8

1 batch of classic shortcrust pastry
   dough or oat pastry dough,
   see recipe page 55
2 handfuls of pecan nuts

FILLING
1 vanilla pod
500 ml (18 fl oz) whipping cream
270 g (9 ½ oz) caster sugar
40 g (1 ½ oz) brown sugar
2 tablespoons honey
150 ml (¼ pint) golden syrup
1 tablespoon good quality cocoa powder
50 g (2 oz) unsalted butter, softened

1. Prepare the dough according to the basic recipe.
2. Preheat the oven to 175°C/350°F/gas 4.
3. Roll out the pastry on lightly floured surface to a circle and use it to line a loose-bottomed pie tin. Prick the base with a fork. Fill the case with foil or beans and bake blind for about 10 minutes.
4. Split the vanilla pod lengthways and scrape out the seeds.
5. Put all ingredients except the butter in a saucepan. Heat, then simmer for about an hour.
6. Use the cold water test described above. When the butterscotch is ready, stir in the butter in knobs.
7. Fill the pie case with butterscotch, sprinkle whole pecans on top and put in the refrigerator to set.

conversion chart

The following conversions have been used throughout the book. They are not always exact equivalents but rounded up or down for convenient measuring. Only use one set of measurements in a recipe, do not mix the two.

SOLID MEASURES

ounces	pounds	grams
¼		5
½		15
¾		20
1		25
1 ¼		30
1 ½		40
2		50
2 ⅓		60
2 ½		65
2 ⅔		70
3		75
3 ½		90
4	¼	100
4 ¼		110
4 ½		120
4 ¾		135
5		150
6		175
6 ¼		180
7		200
7 ½		210
8	½	225
8½		240
9		250
9 ½		270
10		280
11		300
12	¾	350
14		400
15		420
16	1	450
18		500
20	1 ¼	550
24	1 ½	675
28	1 ¾	800
32	2	900
36	2 ¼	1 kg
40	3 ½	2 kg

LIQUID MEASURES

fluid ounces	imperial	millilitres
	1 teaspoon	5
	1 dessertspoon	10
	1 tablespoon	15
1	2 tablespoons	25
2		50
3		75
3 ½		100
4		110
5	¼ pint	150
6		170
7		200
8		250
10	½ pint	300
14		400
15	¾ pint	450
17		500
25	1 ¼ pints	750
30	1 ½ pints	900
50	2 ½ pints	1.5 litres

easy-to-make french fruit flan

I often vary this delicious recipe to make flans with fresh apples, nectarines, plums or apricots. You can also make them with canned peaches or apricots.

MAKES 8 FLANS

8 pieces of puff pasty, each 10 x 20 cm
(4 x 8 in), thawed if frozen
egg for brushing
150 g (5 oz) homemade almond paste,
see recipe page 208 (or use
ready-made marzipan)
4–5 ripe pears or peaches
90 g (3 ½ oz) demerara sugar
2 teaspoons ground cinnamon
4 sprigs of fresh rosemary
1 handful of slivered almonds
cold butter to slice on top of the flans
icing sugar

1. Preheat the oven to 200°C/400°F/gas 6.
2. Use a glass to mark two circles in each pastry sheet, but not all the way through. Use a fork to prick the surface of the circles.
3. Brush the edges of the circles with beaten egg.
4. Grate the almond paste and spread it inside the circles.
5. Core the pears or halve and stone the peaches. Slice the fruit thinly and mix with the demerara sugar, cinnamon and finely chopped rosemary.
6. Arrange the fruit on top of the almond paste in shape of a fan and sprinkle slivered almonds on top.
7. Put thin slices of cold butter on top and bake the flans in the centre of the oven for 20–25 minutes or until golden.
8. Dust the flans with icing sugar.

strawberry flan with toffee cream

These wonderful flans are perfect to make in the summertime. Plenty of pleasure for almost no work.

MAKES 2 FLANS/SERVES 10

250 g (9 oz) fresh puff pastry
egg for brushing
100 g (4 oz) good quality dark chocolate
(70% cocoa solids)
2 batches of butterscotch cream,
see recipe page 211
900 g (2 lb) fresh strawberries, hulled
and sliced

1. Preheat the oven to 175°C/350°F/gas 4.
2. Roll out pastry to a rectangle and cut four strips, each 1 cm (½ in) wide from a long edge. Divide the remaining pastry in half.
3. Line a baking sheet with greaseproof paper. Transfer the two pieces of pastry to the baking sheet and brush the edges with beaten egg. Stick the pastry strips to the long edges.
4. Brush the pastry with egg, prick the centre of the flans with a fork and bake in the centre of the oven for about 25 minutes.
5. Meanwhile, chop the chocolate coarsely and melt it in a bowl set over a pan of simmering water.
6. Brush the freshly baked flans with melted chocolate within the edges.
7. When the chocolate has set, spoon butterscotch cream onto the flans and arrange sliced strawberries on top.

raspberry lemon meringue pie

I top my version of the classic lemon meringue pie with raspberry meringue. The sourness from the lemon and the sweetness of the meringue are perfects partners. When you are making meringue, be careful not to let any of the egg yolk slip into the bowl with the whites. Fat from the yolk will prevent the formation of good foam, and you will end up without any meringue.

MAKES 1 PIE/SERVES 12

1 batch of classic shortcrust pastry
    dough, see recipe page 55
3 batches of lemon curd, see recipe
    page 208
egg for brushing
fresh raspberries for decoration
icing sugar

RASPBERRY MERINGUE

3 organic egg whites
juice of ½ lemon
350 g (11 ½ oz) caster sugar
200 g (7 oz) fresh raspberries

1. Prepare the dough according to the basic recipe.
2. Roll out the pastry on a lighlty floured surface and line a loose-bottomed pie tin. Transfer to the freezer.
3. Preheat the oven to 175°C/350°F/gas 4.
4. Brush the bottom of the frozen crust with beaten egg and prick the bottom of the crust with a fork, then bake blind for about 10 minutes until lightly golden.
5. Fill the pastry case with foil or beans.
6. When the pie case is cool fill it with lemon curd.
7. Increase the oven temperature to 240°C/475°F/gas 9.
8. In a stainless steel bowl, beat together the egg whites, lemon juice and 90 g (3 ½ oz) caster sugar to stiff peaks.
9. Fold in another 90 g (3 ½ oz) caster sugar.
10. Mix the raspberries with the remaining sugar until the raspberries separate. Carefully blend the raspberries in batches into the meringue. Beat the meringue until firmly peaking.
11. Pipe or spread the meringue on top of the pie and bake in the centre of the oven with the oven door ajar for about 5 minutes or until the meringue starts to turn golden.
12. Decorate the pie with fresh raspberries and dust the top with icing sugar.

cupcakes & muffins

The first thing I ever learned to bake was a classic muffin under the supervision of my granny. There are dozens of muffin recipes, and I have collected together my own favourites in this chapter. The cupcake, or fairy cake, is a close and popular cousin to the muffin. The main difference is that cupcakes have icing on top.

classic cupcakes

Cupcakes are a fun alternative to a traditional cake when you are having a party. These sweet little jewels are great with either cream cheese or white chocolate frosting – choose whichever you prefer! I always put the paper cases in a muffin tin because it makes the cupcakes rise to splendid heights.

MAKES 12 CAKES
BASIC RECIPE
3 organic eggs
225 g (8 oz) caster sugar
1 teaspoon vanilla sugar
100 g (4 oz) unsalted butter
100 ml (3 ½ fl oz) milk
210 g (7 ½ oz) plain flour
2 teaspoons baking powder
1 pinch of salt
zest and juice of 1 lemon
sprinkles or crystallised flowers for
    decoration

CREAM CHEESE FROSTING
60 g (2 ½ oz) unsalted butter, softened
300 g (11 oz) icing sugar
1 teaspoon vanilla sugar
1 tablespoon freshly squeezed
    lemon juice
100 g (4 oz) cream cheese
a few drops of food colouring

WHITE CHOCOLATE FROSTING
200 g (7 oz) good quality white chocolate
200 g (7 oz) cream cheese

1. Preheat the oven to 175°C/350°F/gas 4.
2. Beat together the eggs, butter and vanilla sugar until pale and fluffy.
3. Melt the butter, pour in the milk and blend with the egg mixture.
4. Mix together the flour, baking powder and salt and carefully fold into the mixture.
5. Add the lemon zest and juice to the mixture.
6. Put paper cases in a muffin tin and pour in the mixture until the cases are two-thirds full.
7. Bake in the centre of the oven for about 15 minutes. Leave to cool.
8. Make the cream cheese frosting by mixing together the butter, icing sugar, vanilla sugar, lemon juice and cream cheese until creamy.
9. If you want frosting in a few different colours divide the frosting into separate bowls and mix in the chosen food colour or leave it white.
10. Spread the frosting over the cupcakes and decorate with sprinkles or flowers.
11. Alternatively, make white chocolate frosting. Chop the chocolate and melt in a bowl set it over a pan of simmering water. Leave to cool a little.
12. Mix the chocolate with cream cheese and spread it over the cakes.

chocolate cupcakes

MAKES 12 CAKES

BASIC RECIPE

3 organic eggs

225 g (8 oz) caster sugar

1 teaspoon vanilla sugar

50 g (2 oz) unsalted butter

100 ml (3 ½ fl oz) sour cream

2 tablespoons cold coffee

210 g (7 ½ oz) plain flour

2 teaspoons baking powder

4 tablespoons good quality cocoa powder

1 pinch of salt

100 g (4 oz) good quality dark chocolate
    (70% cocoa solids)

sprinkles or crystallised flowers for
    decoration

CHOCOLATE FROSTING

65 g (2 ½ oz) unsalted butter, softened

300 g (11 oz) icing sugar

1 teaspoon vanilla sugar

25 g (1 oz) good quality cocoa powder

100 g (4 oz) cream cheese

1 tablespoon warm coffee

1. Preheat the oven to 175°C/350°F/gas 4.
2. Beat together the eggs, butter and vanilla sugar until pale and fluffy.
3. Melt the butter, add the sour cream and coffee and blend with the egg mixture.
4. Mix together the flour, baking powder, cocoa powder and salt and carefully fold into the mixture.
5. Chop the chocolate coarsely and melt it in a bowl set over a pan of simmering water. Add to the mixture.
6. Put paper cases in a muffin tin and pour in the mixture until the cases are two-thirds full.
7. Bake in the centre of the oven for about 15 minutes. Leave to cool.
8. Make the frosting by mixing together the butter, icing sugar, vanilla sugar, cocoa powder and cream cheese until creamy. Stir in the coffee.
9. Spread the frosting over the cupcakes and decorate with sprinkles or flowers.

raspberry cupcakes

MAKES 12 CAKES

1 batch of classic cupcake mixture,
    see recipe page 85

150 g (5 oz) fresh or frozen raspberries

RASPBERRY FROSTING

180 g (6 ¼ oz) icing sugar

150 g (5 oz) cream cheese

75 g (3 oz) fresh or frozen raspberries,
    and extra for decoration

1. Prepare the mixture according to the basic recipe and carefully blend in the raspberries.
2. Put paper cases in a muffin tin and pour in the mixture until the cases are two-thirds full.
3. Bake in the centre of the preheated oven for about 15 minutes. Leave to cool.
4. Make the frosting by mixing together the icing sugar and cream cheese until creamy.
5. Carefully blend in the raspberries and spread the frosting over the cupcakes.
6. Decorate with fresh raspberries.

lemon poppy seed cupcakes

A cupcake mixture is traditionally a bit denser than a muffin mixture. I mix the mixture thoroughly until it's smooth before filling the paper cases. Lemon and poppy seeds are a brilliant mix, and I discovered this delightful yet sour innovation when I lived in New York. They soon became my favourites, and I never get tired of these wonderful, fresh cupcakes. Try them and you won't be disappointed!

MAKES 12 CAKES

1 batch of classic cupcake mixture,
    see recipe page 85
65 g (2 ½ oz) poppy seeds
zest of 2 lemons
juice of 1 lemon
poppy seeds and whitecurrants for
    decoration

LEMON CREAM CHEESE FROSTING

65 g (2 ½ oz) soft butter
300 g (11 oz) icing sugar
1 teaspoon vanilla sugar
zest of 2 lemons
juice of ½ lemon
100 g (4 oz) cream cheese

1. Prepare the mixture according to the basic recipe. Add the poppy seeds and the additional lemon zest and lemon juice.
2. Put paper cases in a muffin tin and pour in the mixture until the cases are two-thirds full.
3. Bake in the centre of the preheated oven for about 15 minutes. Leave to cool.
4. Make the frosting by mixing together the butter, icing sugar, vanilla sugar, lemon zest, lemon juice and cream cheese until creamy.
5. Spread the frosting over the cupcakes and decorate with poppy seeds and whitecurrants.

banana fudge cupcakes

MAKES 12 CAKES

1 batch of chocolate cupcake mixture,
   see recipe page 86
2 bananas, sliced
1 tablespoon ground cinnamon
coloured sweets for decoration

CHOCOLATE FUDGE ICING

150 ml (¼ pint) whipping cream
2 tablespoons honey
4 tablespoons brown sugar
1 teaspoon ground ginger
15 g (½ oz) unsalted butter
200 g (7 oz) good quality dark chocolate
   (70% cocoa solids)

1. Prepare the mixture according to the basic recipe and add the sliced bananas and cinnamon.
2. Put paper cases in a muffin tin and pour in the mixture until the cases are two-thirds full.
3. Bake in the centre of the preheated oven for about 15 minutes. Leave to cool.
4. Make the icing by bringing the whipping cream, honey, brown sugar and ginger to the boil. Leave to cool a little.
5. Add the butter and finely chopped chocolate and stir until it melts.
6. Leave the mixture to cool slightly before icing the cupcakes.
7. Decorate with sweets.

blueberry corn muffins

These substantial corn and blueberry muffins are wonderful to eat warm and freshly baked with some butter and flaked salt on top – yummy!

MAKES 12 CAKES

100 g (4 oz) unsalted butter
2 organic eggs
150 ml (¼ pint) buttermilk
180 g (6 ¼ oz) plain flour
150 g (5 oz) polenta
150 g (5 oz) caster sugar
1 teaspoon baking powder
1 pinch of salt
1 tablespoon plain flour for the
   blueberries
150 g (5 oz) fresh or frozen blueberries
demerara sugar

1. Preheat the oven to 220°C/425°F/gas 7.
2. Melt the butter and beat it with eggs and buttermilk.
3. Mix the flour, polenta, sugar, baking powder and salt in a bowl.
4. Pour the dry ingredients into the egg mixture and fold in carefully. Don't worry if there are small lumps of flour in the mixture.
5. Toss the blueberries in the flour and carefully mix into the mixture.
6. Put paper cases in a muffin tin and pour in the mixture until the cases are two-thirds full.
7. Sprinkle demerara sugar on top of each muffin and bake in the centre of the oven for about 20 minutes or until a skewer inserted into the centre comes out clean.

peanut butter cupcakes

There are loads of delicious frostings you can use to ice your cupcakes, and there are no limits to how you decorate them. This frosting is as tasty as it is simple to make.

MAKES 12 CAKES

1 batch of chocolate cupcake mixture,
   see recipe page 86
150 g (5 oz) salted peanuts and extra for
   decoration

PEANUT BUTTER FROSTING

100 g (4 oz) soft peanut butter
240 g (8 ½ oz) icing sugar
4 tablespoons good quality cocoa
   powder
2 teaspoons vanilla sugar
150 g (5 oz) cream cheese
1 tablespoon warm coffee

1. Prepare the mixture according to the basic recipe.
2. Put paper cases in a muffin tin.
3. Chop the peanuts and add them to the paper cases, layering them with the cake batter until two-thirds full.
4. Bake in the centre of the preheated oven for about 15 minutes. Leave to cool.
5. Stir the peanut butter, icing sugar, cocoa powder, vanilla sugar and cream cheese until creamy. Stir in the coffee.
6. Spread the frosting on top of the cakes and decorate with extra peanuts.

carrot, ginger, walnut cupcakes

When it comes to carrot cupcakes the key to success is to put lots of flavour into the mixture. I like ginger, but you can vary the flavouring and use ground cloves or allspice instead.

MAKES 12 CAKES

3 organic eggs
270 g (9 ½ oz) caster sugar
180 g (6 ¼ oz) plain flour
1 teaspoon vanilla sugar
3 teaspoons baking powder
1 pinch of salt
1 ½ teaspoons ground cinnamon
1 teaspoon ground cardamom
2 teaspoons ground ginger
150 ml (¼ pint) sunflower oil
450 g (1 lb) grated carrots
100 g (4 oz) walnuts chopped
whole walnuts for decoration

CREAM CHEESE LIME FROSTING

65 g (2 ½ oz) soft butter
300 g (11 oz) icing sugar
1 teaspoon vanilla sugar
zest of 1 lime
100 g (4 oz) cream cheese

1. Preheat the oven to 175°C/350°F/gas 4.
2. Beat the eggs and the sugar until pale and fluffy.
3. Mix together the dry ingredients and fold into the egg mixture.
4. Stir in the oil, carrots and coarsely chopped walnuts.
5. Put paper cases in a muffin tin and pour in the mixture until the cases are two-thirds full.
6. Bake in the centre of the oven for 12–15 minutes. Leave to cool.
7. Make the frosting by mixing together the ingredients until creamy.
8. Spread the frosting on top of the cupcakes and decorate each one with a whole walnut.

high-hat cupcakes

These fantastic-looking cupcakes should be served cold. You can keep them in the refrigerator for about three days, but cover them carefully in clingfilm to keep them fresh. They are the yummiest of cupcakes.

MAKES 12 CAKES

1 batch of chocolate cupcake mixture,
   see recipe page 86

MERINGUE TOPPING

6 organic egg whites
850 g (1 ¾ lb) caster sugar
juice of 1 lemon
2 teaspoons vanilla sugar

CHOCOLATE COATING

350 g (12 oz) good quality dark chocolate
   (70% cocoa solids)
3 tablespoons vegetable oil

1. Prepare the cupcakes according to the basic recipe. Bake them in the preheated oven for 15 minutes. Leave to cool.
2. In a stainless steel bowl mix together the egg whites, caster sugar and lemon juice. Beat by hand for about 1 minute until fluffy.
3. Rest the bowl over a pan of boiling water. Beat until the sugar crystals have dissolved and the mixture has a consistency as fluffy as meringue. You should see the trail from the whisk in the foam.
4. Remove the bowl from the pan and beat the vanilla sugar into the foam. Use a hand-held electric beater to mix the meringue for a few minutes until it is thick and cool.
5. Put the meringue in a piping bag with a round nozzle and pipe the meringue on top of the cupcakes spirals. Leave about in 1 cm (½ in) around the edges.
6. Leave to set in the refrigerator.
7. Make the coating. Chop the chocolate and melt it with vegetable oil in a bowl set over a pan of simmering water.
8. Pour the chocolate into a small bowl and leave to cool.
9. Take the cupcakes out of the fridge and dip each peak in the chocolate. Brush on additional chocolate if there are any gaps.
10. Leave to set on a plate in the refrigerator for about 30 minutes.

nine classic muffins

When I'm baking muffins, I mix the dry ingredients and the liquids separately. Then I blend everything together quickly, without stirring too much. Don't worry if there are small lumps of flour in the mixture the muffins will still turn out gorgeously fluffy and amazingly moist.

MAKES 6 LARGE/12 SMALL
   MUFFINS
BASIC RECIPE
100 g (4 oz) unsalted butter
200 ml (7 fl oz) milk
zest of 1 lemon
2 organic eggs
150 g (5 oz) caster sugar
1 teaspoon vanilla sugar
240 g (8 ½ oz) plain flour
2 teaspoons baking powder
1 pinch of salt

1. Preheat the oven to 175°C/350°F/gas 4 for large muffins and 200°C/400°F/gas 6 if you want to make small muffins.
2. Melt the butter and add the milk and lemon zest.
3. Beat together the eggs, caster sugar and vanilla sugar until pale and fluffy.
4. Stir the butter mixture into the egg mixture.
5. Mix together the flour, baking powder and salt and carefully fold into the mixture.
6. Put paper cases in a muffin tin and pour in the mixture until the cases are two-thirds full.
7. Bake in the centre of the oven for about 20 minutes for large muffins or 12–15 minutes for small ones. A skewer inserted into the centre should come out clean.

malteser muffins

MAKES 6 LARGE/12 SMALL
   MUFFINS
1 batch of muffin mixture, see basic
   recipe above and instructions
50 g (2 oz) unsalted butter (extra)
50 g (2 oz) good quality cocoa powder
   (instead of 50 g/2 oz plain flour)
200 ml (7 fl oz) sour cream (instead of
   milk)
1 bag of Maltesers

1. Prepare the muffin mixture according to the basic recipe but add 50 g (2 oz) extra butter, replace 50 g (2 oz) of the flour with cocoa powder and use sour cream instead of the milk.
2. Put paper cases in a muffin tin and pour in the mixture until the cases are two-thirds full.
3. Stick a few Maltesers in every muffin and bake in the centre of the preheated oven for about 20 minutes for large muffins or 12–15 minutes for small ones.

forest berry muffins

MAKES 6 LARGE/12 SMALL
   MUFFINS
1 batch of muffin mixture, see basic
   recipe above
135 g (4 ¾ oz) fresh or frozen
   blueberries, blackberries and
   raspberries

1. Prepare the muffin mixture according to the basic recipe.
2. Put paper cases in a muffin tin. Layer the berries with the muffin batter until the paper cases are two-thirds full.
3. Bake in the centre of the preheated oven for about 20 minutes for large muffins or 12–15 minutes for small ones.

cherry muffins

MAKES 6 LARGE/12 SMALL
MUFFINS

1 batch of muffin mixture, see basic
recipe page 98
270 g (9 ½ oz) fresh cherries

1. Prepare the muffin mixture according to the basic recipe.
2. Wash and pit cherries.
3. Put paper cases in a muffin tin. Layer the cherries and muffin batter in the paper cases until they are two-thirds full.
4. Bake in the centre of the preheated oven for about 20 minutes for large muffins or 12–15 minutes for small ones.

orange chocolate muffins

MAKES 6 LARGE/12 SMALL
MUFFINS

1 batch of muffin mixture, see basic
recipe page 98
zest of 2 oranges
200 g (7 oz) chocolate and orange
crunch

1. Prepare the muffin mixture according to the basic recipe and add the orange zest.
2. Put paper cases in a muffin tin and carefully pour in the mixture until the cases are two-thirds full.
3. Add a few pieces of chocolate and orange cruch to each muffin.
4. Bake in the centre of the preheated oven for about 20 minutes for large muffins or 12–15 minutes for small ones.

banana chocolate chip muffins

MAKES 6 LARGE/12 SMALL
MUFFINS

1 batch of muffin mixture, see basic
recipe page 98 and instructions
50 g (2 oz) unsalted butter (extra)
50 g (2 oz) good quality cocoa powder
(instead of 65 g (2 ½ oz) plain flour)
200 ml (7 fl oz) sour cream (instead of
milk)
3 ripe bananas
200 g (7 oz) good quality dark chocolate
(70% cocoa solids)

1. Prepare the muffin mixture according to the basic recipe but add 50 g (2 oz) extra butter, replace 65 g (2 ½ oz) flour with cocoa powder and replace the milk with sour cream.
2. Put paper cases in a muffin tin.
3. Slice the bananas and chop the chocolate coarsely. Reserving some of the chocolate pieces for decoration, layer the banana, chocolate and muffin batter in the paper cases until they are two-thirds full.
4. Bake in the centre of the preheated oven for about 20 minutes for large muffins or 12–15 minutes for small ones.

snickers muffins

MAKES 6 LARGE/12 SMALL
MUFFINS

1 batch of muffin mixture, see basic
recipe page 98
1 bag of mini Snickers

1. Prepare the muffin mixture according to the basic recipe.
2. Put paper cases in a muffin tin and carefully pour in the mixture until the cases are two-thirds full.
3. Stick a few mini Snickers in each muffin and bake in the centre of the preheated oven for about 20 minutes for large muffins or 12–15 minutes for small ones.

pineapple muffins with coconut & lime

MAKES 6 LARGE/12 SMALL
MUFFINS
1 batch of muffin mixture, see basic
recipe page 98
½ fresh or canned pineapple
90 g (3 ½ oz) desiccated coconut
zest of 3 limes

1. Prepare the muffin mixture according to the basic recipe.
2. Remove the skin and core from the pineapple and cut the flesh in pieces. If you use canned pineapple cut the rings in pieces.
3. Toast the desiccated coconut in a dry saucepan, reserving 45 g (1 ¾ oz) for decoration.
4. Add the pineapple, roasted desiccated coconut and lime zest to the mixture and stir to combine.
5. Put paper cases in a muffin tin and carefully pour in the mixture until the cases are two-thirds full. Sprinkle each muffin with the reserved desiccated coconut.
6. Bake in the centre of the preheated oven for about 20 minutes for large muffins or 12–15 minutes for small ones.

cinnamon & ginger muffins

MAKES 6 LARGE/12 SMALL
MUFFINS
1 batch of muffin mixture, see basic
recipe page 98
2 teaspoons ground cinnamon
1 teaspoon ground ginger
2 teaspoons ground clove
2 handfuls of slivered almonds
2 teaspoons orange zest

1. Prepare the muffin mixture according to the basic muffin recipe but bring the spices to the boil with milk. Leave the milk to cool before you blend it in the mixture.
2. Toast 2/3 of the slivered almonds in a dry saucepan.
3. Blend slivered almonds and orange zest the mixture.
4. Place paper cases in a muffin tin and carefully pour in the mixture until the cases are two-thirds full.
5. Sprinkle the unroasted slivered almonds on top of the muffins.
6. Bake in the centre of the preheated oven for about 20 minutes for large muffins or 12–15 minutes for small ones.

wild strawberry & cardamom muffins

MAKES 6 LARGE/12 SMALL
MUFFINS
2 tablespoons cardamom pods
1 batch of muffin mixture, see basic
recipe page 98
90 g (3 ½ oz) fresh wild strawberries
1 handful of slivered almonds

1. Pound the cardamom pods in a mortar. Put the milk in a saucepan, add the cardamom and bring to the boil. Leave to infuse. When the milk is cool prepare the mixture according to the basic muffin recipe.
2. Put paper cases in a muffin tin. Layer the strawberries with the muffin batter until the cases are two-thirds full.
3. Sprinkle slivered almonds on top of the muffins.
4. Bake in the centre of the preheated oven for about 20 minutes for large muffins or 12–15 minutes for small ones.

cupcakes & muffins

blueberry muffins with crumble

These are definitely my favourite muffins. They are like an unbelievably juicy combination of muffins and crumble.

MAKES 6 LARGE MUFFINS

1 batch of muffin mixture, see basic recipe page 98

230 g (8 ½ oz) fresh or frozen blueberries

CRUMBLE

75 g (3 oz) cold unsalted butter

80 g (3 ¼ oz) rolled oats

65 g (2 ½ oz) plain flour

90 g (3 ½ oz) caster sugar

1. Preheat the oven to 175ºC/350ºF/gas 4.
2. Prepare the muffin mixture according to the basic muffin recipe.
3. Put paper cases in a muffin tin. Reserving some of the blueberries for decoration, layer the berries and muffin battter in the paper cases until they are two-thirds full.
4. Make the crumble. Dice the butter and put it in a bowl with the oats, flour and sugar. Mix it with your fingertips to make breadcrumbs.
5. Sprinkle some of the crumble on top of each muffin and decorate with reserved blueberries.
6. Bake for about 20 minutes in the centre of the oven.

apple cinnamon muffins with crumble

MAKES 6 LARGE MUFFINS

1 batch of muffin mixture, see basic recipe page 98

4 large dessert apples

2 tablespoons butter

2 tablespoons caster sugar

1 tablespoon cinnamon

CRUMBLE

75 g (3 oz) cold unsalted butter

80 g (3 ¼ oz) rolled oats

65 g (2 ½ oz) plain flour

90 g (3 ½ oz) caster sugar

1. Preheat the oven to 175ºC/350ºF/gas 4.
2. Prepare the muffin mixture according to the basic muffin recipe.
3. Remove the cores from the apples and cut into slices. Fry the apples with the butter, sugar and cinnamon in a hot pan for a few minutes. Leave to cool.
4. Put paper cases in a muffin tin. Reserving six apple slices for decoration, mix the remainder with the muffin batter and fill the paper cases to two-thirds full.
5. Make the crumble. Dice the butter and put it in a bowl with the oats, flour and sugar. Mix it with your fingertips to make breadcrumbs.
6. Sprinkle some crumble on top of each muffin and decorate with a slice of apple.
7. Bake for about 20 minutes in the centre of the oven.

brownie cupcakes

MAKES 16 MUFFINS

2 organic eggs
180 g (6 ¼ oz) caster sugar
1 teaspoon vanilla sugar
50 g (2 oz) butter
50 ml (2 fl oz) cooking oil
100 ml (3 ½ fl oz) golden syrup
120 g (4 ½ oz) plain flour
50 g (2 oz) good quality cocoa powder
1 teaspoon baking powder
1 pinch of salt
100 g (4 oz) good quality dark chocolate
    (70% cocoa solids)
Whipping cream and fresh berries for
    decoration

1. Preheat the oven to 175°C/350°F/gas 4.
2. Beat together the eggs, sugar and vanilla sugar until pale and fluffy.
3. Melt the butter and mix it with cooking oil and syrup. Stir into the egg mixture.
4. Mix together the flour, cocoa powder, baking powder and salt and carefully fold into the mixture.
5. Chop the chocolate and melt it in a bowl set over a pan of simmering water. Blend it into the mixture.
6. Put paper cases in a muffin tin and carefully pour in the mixture until the cases are two-thirds full.
7. Bake for about 12 minutes in the centre of the oven. The muffins will fall flat in the centre when removed from the oven.
8. Decorate with lightly whipped cream and fresh berries.

spanish meringue

I got the idea to colour meringues from a patisserie in Barcelona. They had meringues in lots of fun pastel colours. You can vary these classic meringues with different flavourings. For example, it's delicious to mix in roasted slivered almonds in the meringues.

MAKES 9 MERINGUES

7 organic egg whites

525 g (1 ¼ lb) caster sugar

juice of 1 lemon

100 g (4 oz) good quality dark chocolate (70% cocoa solids) or red food colouring

1. Preheat the oven to 120°C/250°F/gas ½.
2. Mix together the egg whites, sugar and lemon juice in a stainless steel bowl.
3. Place the bowl over a pan of simmering water. Beat by hand until the sugar crystals have dissolved and the meringue is 60–65°C(140–155°F).
4. Take the bowl from the pan and beat the meringue with a hand-held electric mixer until the meringue is thick and has cooled.
5. For chocolatey meringues, melt the chopped chocolate in a bowl set over a pan of simmering water and carefully blend it into the meringue to make it striped. To make pink meringues beat about 10 drops of red food colouring into the meringue and blend until it is an even pink colour.
6. Use two teaspoons to drop the mixture into paper cases or onto a baking sheet covered with greaseproof paper.
7. Bake in the centre of the oven for about 1 hour. The meringues should be a bit chewy in the centre when they are cooked.

party cakes

Nothing makes a party more than a cake. My favourites are those with berries, although I also love the Swedish classics Almond Tosca and Princess Cake. Ideally, a cake should be quick and easy to make, but some of these recipes do require a little more time and patience because they have to be made in stages. One tip is to read through the whole recipe carefully before you start. This will give you a sense of the timing and will prepare you for the task ahead.

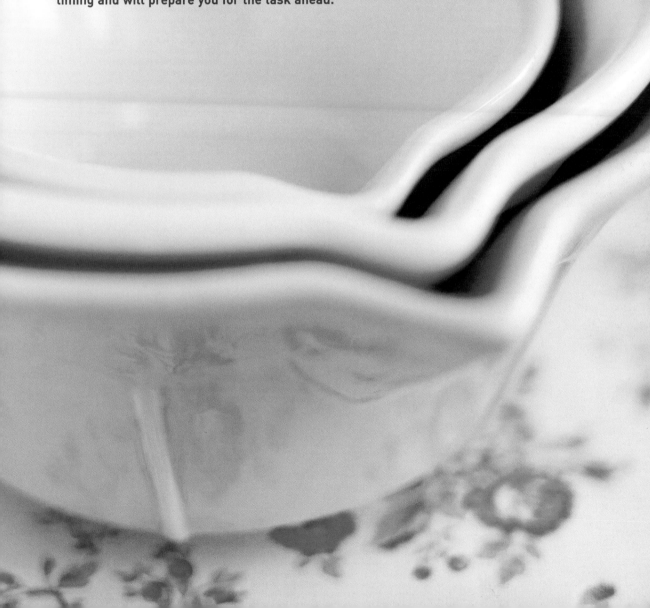

It is easier to construct this cake if you push a skewer through the two lower tiers to hold them together. Allow the meringue cream and chocolate mousse to set a little by cooling them in the fridge for a while before you assemble the cake because this will make them easier to spread.

my most romantic wedding cake

Making a wedding cake is never easy, and it's probably not a task for the stressed-out and nervous wife or husband-to-be. But if you have a relative who enjoys baking, this beautiful wedding cake is quite simple to make.

MAKES 1 CAKE/SERVES 26

LEMON SPONGE

6 organic eggs

450 g (1 lb) caster sugar

2 teaspoons vanilla sugar

100 g (4 oz) unsalted butter and extra
    for greasing the cake tins

200 ml (7 fl oz) milk

420 g (15 oz) plain flour

1 tablespoon baking powder

zest and juice of 2 lemons

CHOCOLATE SPONGE

3 organic eggs

225 g (8 oz) caster sugar

1 teaspoon vanilla sugar

50 g (2 oz) butter

100 ml (3 ½ fl oz) sour cream

210 g (7 ½ oz) plain flour

2 teaspoons baking powder

4 tablespoons good quality cocoa powder

100 g (4 oz) good quality dark chocolate
    (70% cocoa solids)

2 tablespoons cold coffee

WHITE CHOCOLATE MOUSSE

150 g (5 oz) good quality white chocolate

200 ml (7 fl oz) whipping cream

250 ml (8 fl oz) curd cheese

zest of 1 lemon

1. Preheat the oven to 175°C/350°F/gas 4.

2. Make the lemon sponge. Beat together the eggs, sugar and vanilla sugar until pale and fluffy.

3. Melt the butter and stir in the milk. Add to the egg mixture.

4. Mix together the flour and baking powder and carefully fold into the mixture. Stir in the lemon zest and juice.

5. Butter one 25 cm (10 in) and three 15 cm (6 in) nonstick cake tins.

6. Pour half of the mixture into the big tin and distribute the rest into the small tins. Bake in the centre of the oven for 15–20 minutes or until a skewer inserted into the centre comes out clean.

7. Make the chocolate sponge. Beat together the eggs, sugar and vanilla sugar until pale and fluffy.

8. Melt the butter and stir in the sour cream. Add to the egg mixture.

9. Mix together the flour, baking powder and cocoa powder and carefully fold into the mixture.

10. Melt the chocolate in a bowl set over a pan of simmering water. Stir the chocolate and the coffee into the mixture.

11. Butter one 25 cm (10 in) and one 15 cm (6 in) nonstick cake tin.

12. Pour two-thirds of the mixture into larger big tin and the rest into the small tin.

13. Bake in the centre of the preheated oven for 15–20 minutes or until a skewer inserted into the centre comes out clean.

14. Make the white chocolate mousse. Chop the chocolate and melt it in a bowl set over a pan of simmering water.

15. Whip the cream. Blend the curd cheese and the lemon zest into the cream.

16. Blend the cream and curd cheese mixture into the chocolate a little at a time and stir until the mousse is smooth.

(continued on next page)

party cakes

111

DARK CHOCOLATE MOUSSE

100 g (4 oz) good quality dark chocolate
    (70% cocoa solids)
1 organic egg yolk
1 tablespoon dark muscovado sugar
½ teaspoon warm coffee
1 tablespoon dark rum
zest and juice of 1 orange
150 ml (¼ pint) whipping cream

WHITE MERINGUE CREAM

4 organic egg whites
270 g (9 ½ oz) caster sugar
juice of 1 lemon
350 g (12 oz) unsalted butter, softened

ASSEMBLING

1 batch of syrup, see recipe page 210
3 tablespoons dark rum
135 g (4 ¾ oz) fresh raspberries
150 g (5 oz) whitecurrants

17. Make the dark chocolate mousse. Chop the chocolate coarsely and melt it in a bowl set over a pan of simmering water.
18. Beat together the egg yolk and the sugar until creamy. Stir in the coffee, rum, orange zest and juice.
19. Mix the warm, melted chocolate into the egg mixture. Whip the cream lightly (it should be thickening but still runny) and blend it a little at a time into the chocolate mixture.
20. Leave the mousse to set slightly in the refrigerator.
21. Make the meringue cream. Mix together the egg whites, sugar and lemon juice in a stainless steel bowl.
22. Place the bowl over a pan of boiling water. Beat until the mixture thickens, the sugar crystals have dissolved and the meringue is 60–65°C (140–155°F).
23. Remove the bowl from the heat and beat the meringue with a hand-held electric mixer, gradually adding the butter, until it is smooth and cool.
24. Leave the meringue to set in the refrigerator.
25. Cut the large lemon sponge in half horizontally. Trim the top of the large chocolate sponge to make it level.
26. Place one of the lemon sponge layers on a cake stand. Mix the syrup with the rum and brush the surface of the cake with the mixture.
27. Fill a piping bag with meringue and pipe a circle of meringue around the edge. Fill the centre with white chocolate mousse.
28. Put the large chocolate cake on top and brush with the syrup and rum.
29. Pipe a circle of meringue around the edge. Fill the centre with dark chocolate mousse and press some fresh raspberries into the mousse.
30. Put the second large lemon layer on top and cover it with a thin layer of meringue.
31. Trim two of the small lemon sponges to make two layers, each about 1.5 cm (¾ in) thick. Trim the small chocolate cake in the same way.
32. Layer the small lemon and chocolate cakes together, repeating steps 26-30.
33. From the last lemon sponge cut out two small cakes with a glass or a biscuit cutter.
34. Put one of the small cakes on top of the cake and pipe a circle of meringue around the edge. Fill the centre with dark chocolate mousse and raspberries. Put the other small cake on top
35. Cover the whole cake with a thin layer of meringue and arrange currants around each tier.

redberry trifle

Trifle is extremely easy to make, and it makes and impressive and colourful centrepiece at any birthday party. If you want to take a shortcut you can use ready-made sponge.

SERVES 16

1 batch of sponge mixture, see basic
   recipe page 30
400 ml (14 fl oz) whipping cream
500 ml (17 fl oz) low-fat Greek yogurt
100 g (4 oz) homemade almond paste,
   see recipe page 208
100 ml (3 ½ fl oz) Marsala
75 g (3 oz) light muscovado sugar
900 g (2 lb) fresh strawberries
450 g (1 lb) fresh raspberries and
   redcurrants

1. Bake the sponge according to the basic recipe. Use a rectangular cake tin, buttered and covered with breadcrumbs. Leave to cool.
2. Cut the sponge into 1.5 cm (¾ in) slices.
3. Whip the cream and mix it first with the yogurt and then with grated almond paste.
4. Bring the Marsala and the muscovado sugar to the boil. Leave to cool a little.
5. Slice the strawberries and put them together with the berries and currants in the just warm wine.
6. Arrange the cake, fruit and cream in layers in a glass bowl, starting with cake, then fruit, then cream. Finish with a layer of fruit.

mom's swiss roll

This is the simplest and quickest cake in the world, it takes only 5 minutes in the oven. Roll up the cake when it's warm if you are filling it with jam or berries. If you are using hazelnut and chocolate spread or cream for the filling, you should leave it to cool under a tea towel before rolling it, otherwise the filling will melt.

MAKES 1 CAKE
BASIC RECIPE
3 organic eggs
135 g (4 ¾ oz) caster sugar
2 tablespoons milk
zest of 1 orange
120 g (4 ½ oz) plain flour
1 teaspoon baking powder
1 handful slivered almonds
caster sugar for rolling

1. Preheat the oven to 230°C/450°F/gas 8.
2. Beat together the eggs and the sugar until pale and fluffy.
3. Add the milk and the orange zest.
4. Mix the flour with the baking powder and fold into the egg mixture.
5. Spread the mixture thinly and evenly in a Swiss roll tin lined with greaseproof paper.
6. Sprinkle the slivered almonds on top and bake in the centre of the oven for about 5 minutes.
7. Sprinkle sugar on a piece of greaseproof paper and turn out the cake upside down.
8. Carefully loosen the greaseproof paper from the cake base.
9. Fill the cake with a filling of your choice. See variations below and on pages 118-9.

summer cloudberry swiss roll

MAKES 1 CAKE
1 batch of Mom's Swiss Roll, see basic recipe above
45 g (1 ¾ oz) caster sugar
500 g (1 ¼ lb) fresh or frozen cloudberries
50 ml (2 fl oz) cloudberry jam

1. Prepare and cook the cake according to the basic recipe.
2. Mix together the caster sugar and the cloudberries and drain away excess liquid.
3. Mix the berries with the jam and spread the filling over the cake in an even layer.
4. Roll the cake from one long side towards the other, making sure you tuck in the first long side tightly.
5. Cut the cake into 1 cm (½ in) thick slices.

forest berry swiss roll

MAKES 1 CAKE
1 batch of Mom's Swiss Roll, see basic recipe above
450 g (1 lb) mixed fresh or frozen blueberries, blackberries and raspberries
75 g (3 oz) muscovado sugar

1. Prepare and cook the cake according to the basic recipe.
2. Mix together the muscovado sugar and the berries and drain away excess liquid.
3. Spread the fruit evenly over the cake.
4. Roll the cake from one long side towards the other, making sure you tuck in the first long side tightly.
5. Cut the cake into 1 cm (½ in) thick slices.

party cakes

117

almond and amaretto swiss roll

MAKES 1 CAKE

1 batch of Mom's Swiss Roll, see basic
   recipe page 117
3 tablespoons Amaretto liqueur
1 batch of syrup, see recipe on page 210
200 ml (7 fl oz) whipping cream
100 ml (3 ½ fl oz) low-fat Greek yogurt
150 g (5 oz) homemade almond paste,
   see recipe page 208

1. Prepare and cook the cake according to the basic recipe.
2. Mix the Amaretto with the syrup and brush the mixture over the freshly baked cake.
3. Whip the cream and mix it first with the yogurt and then with grated almond paste.
4. Spread the filling over the cake in an even layer.
5. Roll the cake from one long side towards the other, making sure you tuck in the first long side tightly.
6. Cut the cake into 1 cm (½ in) thick slices.

chocolate & banana swiss roll

MAKES 1 CAKE

1 batch of Mom's Swiss Roll, see basic
   recipe page 117 and instructions
50 g (2 oz) butter
25 g (1 oz) good quality cocoa powder
   (instead of 25 g/1 oz plain flour)
¾ jar of hazelnut and chocolate spread
2 ripe bananas

1. Prepare the cake according to the basic recipe but add an extra 50 g (2 oz) melted butter and replace 25 g (1 oz) of the flour with cocoa powder.
2. Bake the cake for about 4 minutes and turn it out according to the basic recipe. Leave to cool a little.
3. Spread chocolate spread over the freshly baked cake and sprinkle over the thinly sliced bananas.
4. Roll the cake from one long side towards the other, making sure you tuck in the first long side tightly.
5. Cut the cake into 1 cm (½ in) thick slices.

blueberry & lemon swiss roll

MAKES 1 CAKE

1 batch of Mom's Swiss Roll, see basic
   recipe page 117 and instructions
zest of 2 lemons
500 g (1 ¼ lb) fresh or frozen
   blueberries
90 g (3 ½ oz) caster sugar

1. Prepare and cook the cake according to the basic recipe but use lemon zest instead of the orange zest.
2. Mix together the caster sugar and the blueberries and drain away the excess liquid.
3. Spread the fruit over the cake.
4. Roll the cake from one long side towards the other, making sure you tuck in the first long side tightly.
5. Cut the cake into 1 cm (½ in) thick slices.

cardamom swiss roll with red berries

MAKES 1 CAKE

1 batch of Mom's Swiss Roll, see basic
   recipe page 117

90 g (3 ½ oz) fresh or frozen
   redcurrants

450 g (1 lb) fresh strawberries

½ teaspoon cardamom pods

2 tablespoons balsamic vinegar

3 tablespoons demerara sugar

1. Prepare and cook the cake according to the basic recipe.
2. Remove the stalks from the redcurrants and hull and thinly slice the strawberries.
3. Pound the cardamom in a mortar.
4. Mix together the fruit, cardamom, vinegar and sugar. Drain away the excess liquid.
5. Spread the fruit over the cake.
6. Roll the cake from one long side towards the other, making sure you tuck in the first long side tightly.
7. Cut the cake into 1 cm (½ in) thick slices.

jam swiss roll

MAKES 1 CAKE

1 batch of Mom's Swiss Roll, see basic
   recipe page 117

300 ml (½ pint) raspberry jam

1. Prepare and cook the cake according to the basic recipe.
2. Spread the jam evenly over the cake.
3. Roll the cake from one long side towards the other, making sure you tuck in the first long side tightly.
4. Cut the cake into 1 cm (½ in) thick slices.

strawberry & basil swiss roll

MAKES 1 CAKE

1 batch of Mom's Swiss Roll, see basic
   recipe page 117

450 g (1 lb) fresh strawberries

90 g (3 ½ oz) caster sugar

1 bunch of fresh basil

zest of 1 lime

1. Prepare and cook the cake according to the basic recipe.
2. Hull and thinly slice the strawberries and mix with the sugar. Drain away the excess liquid.
3. Mix the chopped basil and lime zest with the strawberries. Spread the filling evenly over the cake.
4. Roll the cake from one long side towards the other, making sure you tuck in the first long side tightly.
5. Cut the cake into 1 cm (½ in) thick slices.

classic light sponge

Use a soft and airy fat-free sponge for patisserie-style cakes like the Princess Cake. You can buy them ready-made but why should you? It's easy to make them yourself, and home-made tastes best!

MAKES 1 CAKE/SERVES 12
BASIC RECIPE
4 organic eggs
135 g (4 ¾ oz) caster sugar
90 g (3 ½ oz) plain flour
butter and dried breadcrumbs for the tin

1. Preheat the oven to 200°C/400°F/gas 6.
2. Beat together the eggs and the sugar until pale fluffy.
3. Fold the flour into the egg mixture.
4. Pour the mixture into a buttered 23 cm (9 in) springform cake tin covered with breadcrumbs.
5. Bake in the centre of the oven for 10–15 minutes or until a skewer inserted into the centre comes out clean.
6. Leave the sponge to cool slightly in the tin and then turn it out on to a plate or a wire rack.

princess cake

When I want to give the Princess Cake a slightly more grown-up taste I mix syrup (see recipe page 210) with Amaretto and brush the mixture over the freshly baked cake layers.

MAKES 1 CAKE/SERVES 12
1 classic cake light sponge, see basic recipe above
1 batch of crème patisserie, see recipe page 209
icing sugar

FILLING
110 g (4 ¼ oz) fresh or frozen raspberries
45 g (1 ⅔ oz) caster sugar
750 ml (1 ¼ pints) whipping cream
400 g (14 oz) pink marzipan (use red or pink food colouring if you can't find pink marzipan)

1. Prepare the cake sponge and the vanilla custard according to the recipes.
2. Cut the cake into three horizontal layers.
3. Use one-third of the crème patisserie to pipe three rounds around the edges of the bottom layer.
4. Mix together the raspberries and sugar and spread the fruit inside the crème patisserie circles.
5. Whip the cream until firm and fluffy. Mix a spoonful of the cream with the crème patisserie and spread some of the mix over the raspberries.
6. Put on the next layer of cake and spread some crème patisserie over the top. Put the last layer in place and spread the remaining crème patisserie on top.
7. Spread the cream over the cake, creating a smooth dome shape.
8. Dust a clean surface with icing sugar and roll out the marzipan.
9. Cover the cake with marzipan trimming the excess around the edges. Dust the cake with icing sugar.

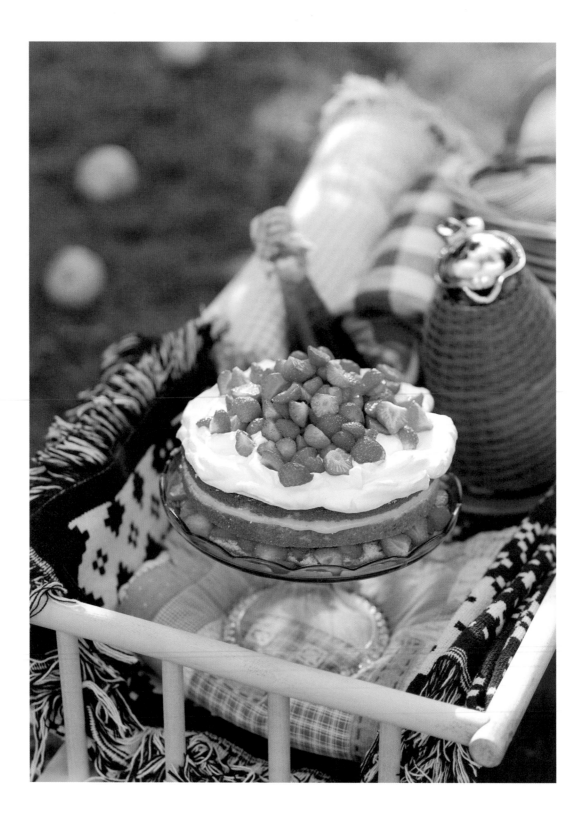

strawberry & lemon curd cake

I like to bake some cakes with a regular sponge since it makes the cake really juicy and yummy. You can mix some syrup (see recipe page 210) with your favourite liqueur and brush the layers to make them extra delicious.

MAKES 1 CAKE/SERVES 12

1 batch of sponge mixture, see basic
   recipe page 30
1 batch of lemon curd, see recipe
   page 208
1 vanilla pod
45 g (1 ¾ oz) caster sugar
900 g (2 lb) fresh strawberries
300 ml (½ pint) whipping cream

1. Prepare the sponge mixture according to the basic recipe and pour it into a buttered 23 cm (9 in) springform cake tin covered with breadcrumbs.
2. Bake in the centre of the oven for about 25 minutes at 175°C/350°F/gas 4.
3. Leave to cool before cutting it into three horizontal layers.
4. Split the vanilla pod lengthways and scrape out the seeds. Mix the seeds with the sugar. Hull and thinly slice half the strawberries and mix them with the sugar.
5. Put a layer of the cake on a serving plate and cover it with the sliced strawberries.
6. Put another layer of cake on the top and spread over the cool lemon curd.
7. Add the final layer of cake. Beat the cream until it is softly peaking and spread it over the top of the cake. Hull and chop the remaining strawberries and pile them on the cream.

aunt elsa's party cake

My Aunt Elsa always makes this smashing party cake for my cousin's birthday. It's easy to vary with different fillings and decorations.

MAKES 1 CAKE/SERVES 12

1 batch of sponge mixture, see basic
   recipe page 30
½ batch of crème patisserie, see recipe
   page 209
100 g (4 oz) fresh or frozen blueberries
100 g (4 oz) fresh or frozen strawberries
2 bananas
90 g (3 ½ oz) caster sugar
300 ml (½ pint) whipping cream

1. Prepare the sponge mixture according to the basic recipe and pour into a buttered 23 cm (9 in) springform cake tin covered with breadcrumbs.
2. Bake in the centre of the oven for about 25 minutes at 175°C/350°F/gas 4.
3. Leave the cake to cool before cutting it into three horizontal layers.
4. Put a layer of the cake on a serving plate and cover it with a layer of cool crème patisserie. Add another layer on top.
5. Mash the berries with the bananas and the sugar. Drain away any excess liquid and spread the fruit over the cake.
6. Put on the top layer of cake and cover the top and sides with lightly whipped cream.

party cakes

gluten-free chocolate & hazelnut torte

This is a superb and moist, gluten-free cake, which you also can use as a basic cake sponge if you want to make a gluten-free party cake. Simply spread chocolate and hazelnut spread and sliced bananas on the cake layers and cover the cake with lightly whipped cream and fresh berries.

MAKES 1 CAKE/SERVES 12

300 g (11 oz) hazelnuts
300 g (11 oz) good quality dark chocolate
    (70% cocoa solids)
1 tablespoon good quality cocoa powder
200 g (7 oz) unsalted butter, softened
90 g (3 ½ oz) caster sugar
6 organic eggs, separated
butter for the cake tin
mixed nuts for decoration

PEANUT BUTTER FROSTING

50 g (2 oz) soft peanut butter
150 g (5 oz) icing sugar
4 tablespoons good quality cocoa
    powder
1 teaspoon vanilla sugar
100 g (4 oz) cream cheese
1 tablespoon warm coffee

1. Preheat the oven to 175°C/350°F/gas 4.
2. Process the hazelnuts in a blender to make a fine powder.
3. Chop 200 g (7 oz) of the chocolate coarsely and mix it in the blender together with the ground hazelnuts.
4. Add the cocoa powder, butter and sugar and mix until creamy.
5. Add the egg yolks to the mixture and continue blending.
6. In a clean, dry bowl beat the egg whites until foaming.
7. Carefully blend the whites into the mixture a little at a time.
8. Pour the mixture into a buttered 23 cm (9 in) springform cake tin covered with breadcrumbs. Break the rest of the chocolate into pieces and push them into the mixture.
9. Bake in the centre of the oven for 30–35 minutes or until a skewer inserted into the centre comes out clean. Remember that the melted pieces of chocolate might make the skewer look sticky even if the cake is ready.
10. Make the frosting. Beat together the peanut butter, icing sugar, cocoa powder, vanilla sugar and cream cheese until creamy. Add the coffee.
11. Spread the frosting on top of the cake and decorate with mixed nuts.

chocolate pavlova

Chocolate Pavlova is a delicious cake that is wonderful when decorated with fresh berries in summer. In winter I use fresh dates and clementines and sprinkle pistachio nuts on top. The cake should be assembled just before serving so that the meringue doesn't go soggy. The original cake is named after the prima ballerina Anna Pavlova who was born in Russia at the end of the nineteenth century.

MAKES 1 CAKE/SERVES 12

7 organic egg whites

500 g (1 ¼ lb) caster sugar

juice of 1 lemon

2 tablespoons good quality cocoa
    powder

50 g (2 oz) slivered almonds

TOPPING

400 ml (14 fl oz) whipping cream

400 ml (14 fl oz) low-fat Greek yogurt

3 tablespoons icing sugar

450 g (1 lb) fresh berries

1. Preheat the oven to 120°C/250°F/gas ½.
2. Beat together the egg whites, sugar and lemon juice in a stainless steel bowl.
3. Place the bowl over a pan of boiling water and continue beating until the mixture thickens, sugar crystals have dissolved and the meringue is 60–65°C (140–155°F).
4. Remove the bowl from heat and use a hand-held electric blender to beat the meringue until it has cooled.
5. Carefully blend the cocoa powder and slivered almonds into the mixture.
6. Cut out a circle of greaseproof paper about 25 cm (10 in) across and put it on a baking sheet. Spoon the meringue onto the paper, using a palette knife to spread it evenly.
7. Bake in the centre of the oven for about 55 minutes. The meringue should be slightly chewy in the centre.
8. Make the topping. Beat together the cream, yogurt and icing sugar. Spread on top of the meringue.
9. Sprinkle fresh berries on top and serve immediately.

three wonderful almond cakes

This moist almond cake is really quick and simple to make. It tastes heavenly and luxurious, just like in a patisserie. It's a perfect birthday cake!

MAKES 1 CAKE/SERVES 12

BASIC RECIPE

250 g (9 oz) unsalted butter, softened

500 g (1 ¼ lb) homemade almond paste, see recipe page 208

5 organic eggs

60 g (2 ⅓ oz) plain flour

butter and slivered almonds for the tin

1. Preheat the oven to 175°C/350°F/gas 4.
2. Beat together the butter and grated almond paste until creamy.
3. Add the eggs, one at a time, beating the mixture after each addition.
4. Carefully fold the flour into the mixture.
5. Butter a 23 cm (9 in) springform cake tin and coat with crushed slivered almonds. Pour in the mixture.
6. Bake in the centre of the oven for about 30 minutes. Finish the cake with a topping of your choice (see variations below).

almond cake with crème patisserie & strawberries

MAKES 1 CAKE/SERVES 12

1 almond cake, see basic recipe above

½ batch of crème patisserie, see recipe page 209

200 ml (7 fl oz) whipping cream

450 g (1 lb) fresh strawberries

1. Prepare the almond cake and crème patisserie according to the recipes. Leave both to cool.
2. Whip the cream until it is firm and fluffy and blend it into the crème patisserie.
3. Hull and chop or slice the strawberries. Spread the crème patisserie over the cake and decorate with the strawberries.

almond cake with elderflower & fresh berries

MAKES 1 CAKE/SERVES 12

1 almond cake, see basic recipe above

1 batch of elderflower custard, see recipe page 210

200 ml (7 fl oz) whipping cream

450 g (1 lb) fresh berries

1. Prepare the almond cake and the elderflower custard according to the recipes. Leave both to cool.
2. Whip the cream until it is softly peaking and blend in the elderflower custard.
3. Spread the custard over the cake and decorate with the berries.

almond tosca cake

MAKES 1 CAKE/SERVES 12

1 almond cake, see basic recipe above

75 ml (3 fl oz) whipping cream

75 g (3 oz) caster sugar

75 ml (3 fl oz) honey

75 g (3 oz) unsalted butter

75 g (3 oz) slivered almonds

1. Prepare the almond cake according to the recipe.
2. Preheat the oven to 200°C/400°F/gas 6.
3. Put the cream, sugar, honey and butter in a saucepan. Bring to the boil, stirring continuously, until the mixture starts to come away from the sides of the saucepan.
4. Stir in the slivered almonds and pour the mixture on top of the almond cake.
5. Bake for 7–10 minutes or until golden. Leave to cool in the tin.

berry squash & buns

My friend Stephen has a lovely expression for happiness. When I call him up and ask him how he's doing, he replies, 'Berry squash and buns' meaning everything's just fine. Squash made from hand-picked berries together with freshly baked buns sum up the Swedish dream of simple, honest, wholesome goodness. I've baked buns since I was knee high, and I reckon there aren't many things that can beat a warm and moist cinnamon bun. Try some of these recipes and you'll get a taste of the Swedish ideal: berry squash and buns!

classic buns

My friend makes the best buns in town, really moist and simply irresistible. When I asked her what her secret was she answered butter. She uses a lot of butter in the dough. I followed her advice and, yes, an instant success! The butter should be at room temperature if you are using a food processor because it will be distributed differently, which makes the dough more elastic and the finished buns wonderfully moist. It's easier to use melted butter if you're mixing the dough by hand, but try using softened butter cut into small pieces for wonderful results.

MAKES 18-24 BUNS/2 CROWNS
BASIC RECIPE
1 tablespoon cardamom pods
300 ml (½ pint) milk
50 g (2 oz) fresh yeast
135 g (4 ¾ oz) caster sugar
½ teaspoon salt
150 g (5 oz) unsalted butter, softened
1 organic egg
660–720 g bread flour

1. Crush the cardamom pods finely in a mortar. Pour the milk into a saucepan add the cardamon and heat until tepid, 38°C (100°F).
2. Sprinkle the yeast into a bowl and dissolve it in the milk, sugar, salt, butter and egg,
3. Add some flour, a little at a time, and mix to a silky and elastic dough.
4. Cover with a tea towel and leave to prove for 45–60 minutes or until doubled in size.
5. Preheat the oven to 200°C/400°F/gas 6.
6. Turn the dough out on to a clean lightly floured surface and make the buns of your choice (see variations).

blueberry buns

MAKES 24 BUNS
1 batch of classic bun dough, see
    basic recipe above
egg for brushing
1 handful of slivered almonds

FILLING
200 g (7 oz) unsalted butter, softened
90 g (3 ½ oz) demerara sugar
1 tablespoon ground cinnamon
110 g (4 ¼ oz) fresh or frozen
    blueberries
2 tablespoons icing sugar
2 tablespoons cornflour

1. Prepare the dough according to the basic recipe.
2. Mix together the butter, demerara sugar and cinnamon until creamy.
3. Divide the dough in half. Roll out one portion on a lightly floured surface to about 1 cm (½ in) thick. Spread half the flavoured butter over the dough.
4. Mix the berries with the icing sugar and cornflour in a bowl. Sprinkle half of the berries over the dough.
5. Roll up the dough as you would a Swiss roll and cut it into pieces 4 – 5 cm (about 2 in) thick. Repeat with the remaining dough and berries.
6. Place in paper cases in a muffin tin or on a baking sheet.
7. Preheat the oven to 200°C/400°F/gas 6.
8. Leave the buns to prove uncovered for 45–60 minutes or until they have doubled in size.
9. Brush with beaten egg and sprinkle slivered almonds on top. Bake in the lower part of the oven for 10 minutes or until golden brown.

apple & almond crown

MAKES 2 CROWNS

1 batch of classic bun dough, see basic
   recipe page 132
egg for brushing
1 of handful slivered almonds

FILLING

200 g (7 oz) unsalted butter, softened
90 g (3 ½ oz) demerara sugar
1 tablespoon ground cinnamon
200 g (7 oz) homemade almond paste,
   see recipe page 208
2 ripe apples

1. Prepare the dough according to the basic recipe.
2. Mix together the butter, demerara sugar, cinnamon and almond paste until creamy.
3. Divide in half. Roll out one portion on a lightly floured surface to a rectangle about 20 x 30 cm (8 x 12 in) and 1 cm (½ in) thick.
4. Spread half of the filling over the dough and sprinkle one grated apple on top. Roll up the dough as you would a Swiss roll and form it into a ring.
5. Butter two 23 cm (9 in) springform cake tins or line two baking sheets with greaseproof paper. Put the dough in a cake tin or on a baking sheet.
6. Cut through the dough, almost to the bottom, at intervals of about 1 cm (½ in) and fold the pieces alternately in and out. Repeat with the remaining ingredients.
7. Preheat the oven to 175°C/350°F/gas 4.
8. Leave the rolls to prove under a tea towel for about 1 hour.
9. Brush with beaten egg and sprinkle slivered almonds on top. Bake for about 20 minutes.

american sticky buns

MAKES 20 BUNS

1 batch of classic bun dough, see basic
   recipe page 132
butter for the tin
egg for brushing
pecan nuts
demerara sugar

FILLING

50 g (2 oz) pecan nuts
50 g (2 oz) walnuts
250 g (9 oz) unsalted butter, softened
110 g (4 ¼ oz) brown sugar
1 tablespoon ground cinnamon
100 g (4 oz) raisins

CREAM CHEESE GLAZE

200 g (7 oz) cream cheese
3 tablespoons golden syrup
90 g (3 ½ oz) icing sugar
zest of 2 limes
juice of 1 lime

1. Prepare the dough according to the basic recipe.
2. Crush the nuts coarsely in a pestle and water and mix with the butter, brown sugar, cinnamon and raisins to a smooth paste.
3. Roll out the dough on a lightly floured surface to a large rectangle. Spread the filling over the dough. Roll up the dough tightly as you would a Swiss roll and cut it into slices about 1.5 cm (¾ in) thick.
4. Place the buns, seam side down, on a buttered baking sheet. Use your thumb to press down in the centre of the buns.
5. Preheat the oven to 200°C/400°F/gas 6.
6. Leave the buns to prove under a tea towel for 45–60 minutes or until they have doubled in size.
7. Brush the buns with beaten egg and sprinkle pecan nuts and demerara sugar on top.
8. Bake in the centre of the oven for about 10 minutes.
9. Mix together the cream cheese, syrup and icing sugar and add the lime zest and juice.
10. Beat the mixture with a hand-held beater until fluffy.
11. Drizzle the glaze over the buns when they have cooled a little.
12. Leave to cool completely and then pull the buns apart.

cardamom buns

These buns will turn out moister if you make a filling by mixing together butter, caster sugar and cinnamon instead of simply sprinkling the spices and sugar directly onto the dough because they will absorb the butter. If you brush your buns with diluted syrup after baking they will look extra shiny and tempting.

MAKES 18 BUNS

1 batch of classic bun dough, see basic
    recipe page 132
egg for brushing
golden syrup and water for brushing
½ tablespoon cardamom pods
45 g (1 ½ oz) caster sugar

FILLING
200 g (7 oz) unsalted butter, softened
90 g (3 ½ oz) caster sugar
1 tablespoon ground cinnamon

1. Prepare the dough according to the basic recipe.
2. Mix together the butter, sugar and cinnamon to make a smooth paste.
3. Divide the dough in half and roll out one portion to a rectangle about 1 cm (½ in) thick.
4. Spread half the filling over the dough and fold the dough in half, long edges together.
5. Cut the sheet into strips about 3.5 cm (1 ½ in) wide and cut almost all the way along the strips (they should look like a pair of trousers).
6. Twist the 'trouser legs' in different directions and tie them in a knot. Make sure the ends are underneath the knot. Place the buns on a baking sheet lined with greaseproof paper.
7. Preheat the oven to 200°C/400°F/gas 6.
8. Leave the buns to prove under a tea towel for about 40 minutes until doubled in size. Brush with beaten egg and bake in the centre of the oven for about 10 minutes or until golden.
9. Brush the still warm buns with syrup mixed with water and sprinkle with ground cardamom mixed with caster sugar.

vanilla buns

You can also make these plain, without any filling, or fill them with apple sauce, cloudberry or blueberry jam.

MAKES 18 BUNS

1 batch of classic bun dough, see basic
    recipe page 132
1 batch of crème patisserie, see recipe
    page 209
butter for brushing
caster sugar

1. Prepare the dough and crème patisserie according to the basic recipes.
2. Divide the dough into 18 pieces and roll each into a ball. Put the balls on a baking sheet lined with greaseproof paper.
3. Flatten them a bit and leave to prove under a tea towel for about 45–60 minutes until doubled in size.
4. Preheat the oven to 200°C/400°F/gas 6.
5. Put the crème patisserie in a piping bag with a round nozzle. and pipe some into each bun.
6. Bake in the centre of the oven for about 7–8 minutes or until golden. Leave to cool a little.
7. Brush the buns with melted butter and roll them in caster sugar.

swedish semlor

MAKES 18 BUNS

1 batch of classic bun dough, see basic
   recipe page 132
egg for brushing
icing sugar

FILLING

400 g (14 oz) homemade almond paste,
   see recipe page 208
milk
900 ml (1 ½ pints) whipping cream

1. Prepare the dough according to the basic recipe.
2. Divide the dough into 18 pieces and roll each into a ball.
3. Put the balls on a baking sheet lined with greaseproof paper.
4. Preheat the oven to 200°C/400°F/gas 6.
5. Leave the buns to prove under a tea towel for about 45–60 minutes.
6. Brush the buns with beaten egg and bake in the centre of the oven for about 6–7 minutes. Leave to cool.
7. Cut the tops off the buns and scoop out the insides.
8. Grate the almond paste and mix with the dough from inside the buns and sufficient milk to make a creamy paste.
9. Stuff the pastries with the filling, pipe whipped cream on top and put the tops back on. Dust the pastries with icing sugar.

bun crackers

Dry buns can be used for two things. Either butter them and throw them on the grill like bruschetta, or make really tasty Bun Crackers. These crackers are delicious crumbled on top of vanilla ice cream or dunked in coffee.

MAKES ABOUT 30 CRACKERS
1 batch of dry cinnamon buns,
   or one crown
butter or margarine for brushing

1. Preheat the oven to 150°C/300°F/gas 2.
2. Cut each bun into slices about 1 cm (½ in) thick.
3. Brush the slices with melted butter or margarine.
4. Place the slices on baking sheets lined with greaseproof paper and cook in the centre of the oven for about 25 minutes until crisp.

brioche pizza with berries

French brioche might not be the healthiest bread you can eat, but it is a real treat and makes wonderful sweet pizzas!

MAKES 16 PIZZAS
1 batch of brioche dough,
   see recipe page 172
1 batch of crème patisserie,
   see recipe page 209
4 ripe nectarines
225 g (8 oz) fresh blackberries or
   raspberries
egg for brushing
demerara sugar

1. Prepare the brioche dough and crème patisserie according to the recipes.
2. Put the dough on a lightly floured surface and roll out gently to a large square. Cut the dough into 16 pieces.
3. Roll each piece into a thin circle and transfer to baking sheets lined with greaseproof paper.
4. Leave the pizzas to prove for 1 hour or until doubled in size.
5. Preheat the oven to 200°C/400°F/gas 6.
6. Pipe a spiral of crème patisserie in the centre of each pizza and top with sliced nectarines and blackberries.
7. Brush the edges with beaten egg and sprinkle some demerara sugar on top. Bake in the centre of the oven for about 8–10 minutes or until golden. Leave to cool on a wire rack.

traditional blackcurrant squash

This is a wonderful and simple squash to make if you have a lot of berries in the garden. The hardest work is probably picking the fruit.

MAKES 2 LITRES (3 ½ PINTS)
450 g (1 lb) fresh blackcurrants
1.5 litres (2 ½ pints) water
270 g (9 ½ oz) caster sugar
1 teaspoon citric acid

1. Rinse the currants thoroughly.
2. Put the fruit in a large stainless steel saucepan and crush them lightly with a potato masher. Add 900 ml (1 ½ pints) water and boil, uncovered, for 10 minutes. Skim off any scum.
3. Strain the squash and add the sugar and citric acid. Return to the saucepan.
4. Stir in the remaining water and slowly bring to the boil again. Skim if necessary.
5. Fill two sterilised bottles to the very top and seal.
6. Store the bottles in a cool place and mix with water to the strength you like, something around one part squash to four parts water.

berry squash & buns

Juice 10.—
Lemonade 15.—
Biscotti 5.—

HORNIMANS TEA

TEXACO
FIRE
CHIEF

lovely lemon lemonade

This lemonade is redolent of the 1950's and American housewives. It's a deliciously refreshing drink and takes only a couple of minutes to knock up.

SERVES 4
juice of 8 lemons
juice of 4 limes
180 g (6 ¼ oz) caster sugar
500 ml (17 fl oz) ice cold water
   or table water
ice cubes and slices of lemon for serving

1. Mix the lemon and lime juices with the sugar in a large jug. Stir to dissolve the sugar.
2. Add the cold water, ice cubes and thinly sliced lemon.

blueberry squash

This recipe is for the enthusiastic berry pickers. Nothing can compare with homemade blueberry squash. It's so simple to make, it almost takes care of itself.

MAKES 2 LITRES (3½ PINTS)
675 g (1 ½ lb) fresh or frozen
   blueberries
1.5 litres (2 ½ pints) water
800 g (1 lb/6 oz) caster sugar
3 teaspoons citric acid

1. Remove any stalks and rinse the blueberries carefully. Thaw the berries if you are using frozen.
2. Mash the berries with a potato masher in a bowl or mix them lightly in a blender.
3. Put the berriers in a non-metallic bowl. Add 900 ml (1 ½ pints) of water, stir and cover with clingfilm. Leave in a cool place, stir from time to time.
4. Transfer to a large saucepan, add the remaining water and bring to the boil, stirring occasionally. Skim if necessary.
5. Strain the squash and add sugar and citric acid.
6. Pour the squash into sterilised bottles up to the very top and seal carefully.
7. Store the bottles in a cool place and mix with water to the strength you like, but around one part squash to four parts water.

elderberry squash

Many people don't realise what a treasure elderberries can be if you use them to make this fantastic squash. Be careful not to mix up common elder with the poisonous red-berried elder or dwarf elder. Common elderberries are black and the trees bloom in early summer while the red-berried elder flowers in late spring.

MAKES 2 LITRES (3 ½ PINTS)
900 g (2 lb) ripe elderberries
3 teaspoons citric acid
1.5 litres (2 ½ pints) water
360 g (12 ½ oz) caster sugar

1. Rinse the berries and put them in a non-metallic bowl. Mash them with a potato masher.
2. Stir in the citric acid and 900 ml (1 ½ pints) water.
3. Cover the bowl with a plate and leave in a cool place for about 24 hours.
4. Transfer the berries to a saucepan, add the remaining water and bring to the boil, skimming if necessary.
5. Strain the squash and add the sugar. Bring the squash to the boil again, stir and skim if necessary.
6. Pour the squash into sterilised bottles up to the very top and seal carefully.
7. Store the bottles in a cool place and mix with water to the strength you like, but around one part squash to four parts water.

elderflower squash

Citric acid exists in a variety of fruits and is extracted from green lemons. In squash, jam and preserves citric acid is used as a preservative and to control the acidity. The citric acid and the sugar together help the pectin in the fruit to set, which is why it is added to jams and pieserves.

MAKES 2 LITRES (3 ½ PINTS)
45 clusters fresh elderflowers
zest and juice of 3 lemons
1.5 litres (2 ½ pints) water
175 g (6 oz) caster sugar
4 teaspoons citric acid

1. Place the elderflowers in a bowl and add lemon zest and juice.
2. Bring the water to the boil and stir in sugar and citric acid. Pour the liquid over the flowers.
3. Cover the bowl with a plate and leave in a cool place for three days. Stir a few times a day.
4. Boil and strain the squash.
5. Pour the squash into sterilised bottles up to the very top and seal carefully.
6. Store the bottles in a cool place and mix with water to the strength you like, but around one part squash to four parts water.

At the end of the summer Swedish people pick up their wicker baskets and head for the forests to harvest blueberries, lingonberries and other local specialities. Try my blueberry buns for a taste of Sweden. We should all make the most of what nature has on offer and use what's at hand in our gardens. Pick blackberries and mix them with a little melted sugar to keep in the freezer – they make a wonderful jam completely free of additives. Perfect on your morning toast or cereal!

strawberry squash

Serve this strawberry squash chilled with ice cubes and decorated with fresh strawberries and slices of lime. It's the best party squash in the world.

MAKES 2 LITRES (3 ½ PINTS)
900 g (2 lb) strawberries
zest and juice of 2 lemons
1 vanilla pod
500 ml (17 fl oz) water
400 g (14 oz) caster sugar
2 teaspoons citric acid

1. Hull and rinse the strawberries. Wash the lemons and peel them with a potato peeler.
2. Halve the vanilla pod lengthways and scrape out the seeds. Chop the strawberries and put them in a stainless steal saucepan with the vanilla seeds and lemon zest and juice.
3. Cover and boil for about 10 minutes. Mash the strawberries against the side of the saucepan and strain the squash through a fine sieve.
4. Return to the saucepan and bring to the boil. Add the sugar and citric acid and stir until the sugar has melted.
5. Pour the squash into sterilised bottles up to the very top and seal carefully.
6. Store the bottles in a cool place and mix with water to the strength you like, but around one part squash to four parts water.

rhubarb squash

If you have a lot of rhubarb growing in your garden, this is an excellent way to use it up. The squash is really simple to make and has a wonderful summery taste.

MAKES 2 LITRES (3 ½ PINTS)
900 g (2 lb) rhubarb sticks
1.5 litres (2 ½ pints) water
450 g (1 lb) caster sugar
2 teaspoons citric acid
juice of 2 lemons

1. Rinse and cut the rhubarbs into small pieces. Put the rhubarb in a saucepan, add the water and boil for about 15 minutes. Don't stir or the squash will be cloudy.
2. Strain the squash and throw away the rhubarb.
3. Return the squash to the saucepan, bring back to the boil and add the sugar, citric acid and lemon juice. Leave to cool.
4. Pour the squash into sterilised bottles up to the very top and seal carefully.
5. Store the bottles in a cool place and mix with water to the strength you like, but around one part squash to four parts water.

savoury bread

For those who are lovers of life there are many ways to indulge your passion. How about a luxurious breakfast in bed? Or why not while away a rainy afternoon with scrumptious teacakes and cheese? Perhaps you'd fancy a picnic in the countryside, lazing under a tree in the sun? And remember, with just one bite you could be whisked off to Italy or Provence! None of this is hard to do: all these bread recipes are simple, and part of the fun is trying out the endless variations.

carrot bread with walnuts

This lovely pull-apart bread is a perfect picnic treat. The spices and the carrots, added for extra moisture, make the bread extra tasty. The salt in the bread has an important function. It strengthens the gluten threads from the flour that keeps the dough together and makes it elastic while it rises. It also gives the bread a crust with a slightly darker colour and a better flavour. Use sea salt if you can; it has a fuller taste.

MAKES 1 LARGE LOAF

250 ml (8 fl oz) milk

250 ml (8 fl oz) freshly squeezed
    carrot juice

50 g (2 oz) fresh yeast

50 ml (2 fl oz) golden syrup

75 g (3 oz) unsalted butter, softened

1 tablespoon salt or sea salt

2 teaspoons ground cloves

2 teaspoons ground ginger

500 g (1 ¼ lb) carrots

100 g (4 oz) walnuts

about 1 kg (2 lb) bread flour

poppy seeds, pumpkin seeds and
    flaked salt

1. Warm the milk and juice until they are tepid (38°C/100°F).
2. Crumble the yeast into a bowl and add the liquid, the syrup, butter, salt and spices.
3. Peel and grate the carrots finely. Chop the walnuts coarsely and blend them into the mixture.
4. Add 600 g (about 1 ¼ lb) of the flour and then add the remainder a little at a time. Knead to make a smooth, elastic dough.
5. Cover the bowl with a tea towel and leave the dough to prove for about 45 minutes or until doubled in size.
6. Turn the dough out on to a floured surface and divide it into three equal portions.
7. Shape one piece into a round loaf and put in the centre of a baking sheet lined with greaseproof paper.
8. Divide all the remaining dough into 14 pieces and shape each piece into a round ball.
9. Place the balls in a circle around the large loaf, positioning them about 1 cm (½ in) apart.
10. Preheat the oven to 200°C/400°F/gas 6.
11. Leave the bread to prove under a tea towel for 30–40 minutes.
12. Brush the bread with water and sprinkle seeds and salt on top.
13. Bake in the bottom of the oven for about 30 minutes or until dark golden. Leave to cool on a wire rack.

savoury bread

tortano

Tortano is a fabulous Italian bread filled with goodies such as prosciutto, olives and mozzarella cheese. It's very filling and perfect for a picnic or as a meal on its own.

MAKES 1 LOAF
15 g (½ oz) fresh yeast
300 ml (½ pint) tepid water
2 tablespoons olive oil
1 tablespoon honey
1 tablespoon flaked salt
150 g (5 oz) durum wheat flour
270 g (9 ½ oz) strong bread flour

FILLING
200 g (7 oz) mozzarella cheese
200 g (7 oz) prosciutto
1 handful of pitted olives
1 bunch of fresh basil

1. Crumble the yeast into a bowl and add in the water, olive oil, honey and salt.
2. Mix in the two flours a little at a time until the ingredients bind together and turn into a smooth elastic dough.
3. Cover the bowl with a tea towel and leave the dough to prove for about 30 minutes.
4. Press the dough into a rectangle about 1 cm (½ in) thick. Don't roll it as then the air trapped in the dough will be squeezed out.
5. Slice the mozzarella cheese and put in layers with the prosciutto, olives and basil on top of the dough.
6. Brush the edges with water and roll up the dough as you would a Swiss roll. Shape it into a circle.
7. Preheat the oven to 250°C/500°F/gas 10.
8. Put the loaf onto a baking sheet lined with greaseproof paper, dust it with flour and leave to prove under a tea towel for about 30 minutes.
9. Put the bread in the oven, then reduce the temperature to 200°C/400°F/gas 6 and bake for 20–25 minutes or until golden brown.

ciabatta classico

MAKES 6 CIABATTAS
25 g (1 oz) fresh yeast
300 ml (½ pint) tepid water
2 tablespoons olive oil
2 teaspoons salt
120 g (4 ½ oz) durum wheat flour
270 g (9 ½ oz) strong bread flour
olive oil for the baking sheet

1. Preheat the oven to 250°C/500°F/gas 10.
2. Crumble the yeast into a bowl and stir in the water and olive oil.
3. Add the salt, durum wheat flour and the bread flour a little at a time until the ingredients bind together and turn into a smooth, elastic dough. Work the dough for 10–15 minutes with the dough hooks on your mixer.
4. Grease a baking sheet with olive oil. Shape the dough into a rectangle about 1.5 cm (¾ in) thick. Dust the dough with flour, put it on the baking sheet and leave it to prove under a tea towel for 30–40 minutes.
5. Divide the bread into 6 rectangles or squares and separate them a little.
6. Put the baking tin in the centre of the oven. Spray some water inside the oven and bake for about 10 minutes.

flour power

Flour is made by grinding grain. There are many different kinds, and they taste and act differently depending on exactly which type of grain you are using and how it has been ground. If it says whole wheat on the packet, the whole grain has been ground, which keeps more of the healthy nutrients in the flour.

Plain flour is made from wheat and is the most common type of flour. It is suitable for most baking and cooking.

Bread flour, or strong flour, is higher in protein and therefore also gluten than plain flour. It can be worked more vigorously into a dough, which makes it ideal for baking bread or preparing pasta. It is not really suitable sponges or biscuits.

Wheatgerm flour is made from the inner part of the grain's kernel. It can be used for bread and cookies and in sauces.

Durum wheat flour is made from a durum wheat that has a harder protein than common wheat, making it suitable for pasta and some types of breads. Durum flour gives a full flavour and good consistency. The inner part of the durum wheat kernel is amber, which makes the flour yellowish. Bread made from durum flour has a distinctive flavour and rusks are crisper, but mix it with plain flour if you are making a cake or your cake may turn out too dense.

Buckwheat flour is not made from a grain but from the seeds of a cereal plant. It is completely free of gluten and is therefore often used as the main ingredient in gluten-free flour.

Graham flour is a whole wheat flour made by grinding the kernel and its contents separately. It is often mixed with plain flour to help the bread to rise. Graham flour is used to make bread, scones and rusks.

Spelt flour is rich in magnesium, vitamin B and iron and can be used in cakes, but it should be combined with bread flour if being used in a dough that should rise. The gluten in spelt is more easily digested and so is easier on the stomach. Whole wheat spelt is also available.

Cornflour is made from ripe maize that is ground into flour. It is used to thicken sauces, pancakes, pies and bread.

Rye flour is a whole grain flour where nothing is removed, which makes it into wholesome and nutritious flour, high in fibre. It is used to make dark breads with a strong rye flavour. If you want your rye bread to rise, you should add some bread flour, which will help this process.

focaccia in seven different ways

I love this Italian bread. It's quick and simple to make and tastes lovely. There are dozens of variations, and it's the perfect bread for the party.

MAKES 2 LOAVES

BASIC RECIPE

25 g (1 oz) fresh yeast

300 ml (½ pint) tepid water

50 ml (2 fl oz) olive oil

2 tablespoons honey

1 tablespoon flaked salt

420–480 g (14 ½ –16 ½ oz) strong bread flour

olive oil and flaked salt for the tray and for the baking

1. Crumble the yeast into a bowl and dissolve it in the water, olive oil, honey and flaked salt.
2. Add the flour a little at a time, work it into a dough and knead for about 5 minutes.
3. Cover the bowl with a tea towel and leave the dough to prove for about 45 minutes or until it has doubled in size.
4. Preheat the oven to 220°C/425°F/gas 7.
5. Turn out the dough onto a floured surface and divide it in two. Knead and shape each piece into a ball, then flatten to about 1 cm (½ in) thick.
6. Grease a baking sheet with olive oil and sprinkle with flaked salt. Put the focaccias on the baking sheet and cover with a tea towel. Leave to prove for about 30 minutes or until doubled in size.
7. Push your fingers into the dough to make holes. Drizzle generously with olive oil and sprinkle with flaked salt. Add any other flavour that you like (see variations below).
8. Bake in the centre of the oven for about 10 minutes or until golden brown.

onion focaccia

MAKES 2 LOAVES

1 batch of focaccia dough, see basic recipe above

3 red onions

olive oil and flaked salt for the tray and for the baking

1. Prepare the dough and leave it to prove on a baking sheet according to the basic recipe.
2. Peel and slice the onions thinly and arrange the onion rings on top of the dough.
3. Push your fingers into the dough to make holes. Drizzle generously with olive oil and sprinkle over flaked salt. Cook as above.

olive & fennel focaccia

MAKES 2 LOAVES

1 batch of focaccia dough, see basic recipe above

200 g (7 oz) pitted black olives

2 tablespoons fennel seed

olive oil and flaked salt for the tray and for the baking

1. Prepare the dough and leave it to prove on a baking sheet according to the basic recipe.
2. Chop the olives finely and pound the fennel seed in a mortar. Sprinkle olives and crushed fennel seed on top of the dough.
3. Push your fingers into the dough to make holes. Drizzle generously with olive oil and sprinkle over flaked salt. Cook as above.

rosemary focaccia

MAKES 2 LOAVES

1 batch of focaccia dough, see basic
    recipe page 161
5 sprigs of rosemary
olive oil and flaked salt for the baking
    sheet and for the baking

1. Prepare the dough and leave it to prove on a baking sheet according to the basic recipe.
2. Pound the rosemary sprigs in a mortar. Pour some olive oil into the mortar and pound together with the rosemary.
3. Push your fingers into the dough to make holes. Sprinkle rosemary over the dough.
4. Drizzle generously with olive oil and sprinkle with flaked salt. Cook as above.

potato & goat cheese focaccia

MAKES 2 LOAVES

1 batch of focaccia dough, see basic
    recipe page 161
2 large new potatoes
1 garlic clove
2 sprigs of rosemary
200 g (7 oz) goats cheese
olive oil and flaked salt for the baking
    sheet and for the baking

1. Prepare the dough and leave it to prove on a baking sheet according to the basic recipe.
2. Wash the potatoes and slice potatoes and garlic paper-thin.
3. Spread potatoes, garlic, some flaked salt, chopped rosemary and crumbled goat cheese on top of the dough.
4. Push your fingers into the dough to make holes in the foccacia and make the potatoes, cheese and garlic penetrate. Drizzle generously with olive oil and sprinkle with flaked salt. Cook as above.

parmesan focaccia

MAKES 2 LOAVES

1 batch of focaccia dough, see basic
    recipe page 161
150 g (5 oz) Parmesan cheese
olive oil and flaked salt for the baking
    sheet and for the baking

1. Prepare the dough and leave it to prove on a baking sheet according to the basic recipe.
2. Grate the Parmesan cheese coarsely and spread it on top of the dough.
3. Push your fingers into the dough to make holes. Drizzle generously with olive oil and sprinkle with flaked salt. Cook as above.

focaccia with cherry tomatoes & basil

MAKES 2 LOAVES

1 batch of focaccia dough, see basic
    recipe page 161
1 stem of cherry tomatoes
1 bunch of fresh basil
olive oil and flaked salt for the baking
    sheet and for the baking

1. Prepare the dough and leave it to prove on a baking sheet according to the basic recipe.
2. Push your fingers into the dough to make holes.
3. Press tomatoes and basil into the dough. Drizzle generously with olive oil and sprinkle with flaked salt. Cook as above.

Is there anything better than waking up to the smell of freshly baked bread and a breakfast in bed? I love travelling and staying at a cosy hotel or bed and breakfast. A really good hotel breakfast is high on my list of priorities so I choose my destinations and hotels carefully. Sometimes such treasures are closer to home than you may think. The morning hour yields golden flour.

Welcome in my Garden, please shut the gate.

baguettes

We associate the baguette with France, but actually the French didn't start to bake it until the 1920s. That was when Austrian journeymen brought a Polish method using sourdough to France and started to use this for baking baguettes. The approach gives the baguette its typical light structure containing large air bubbles.

MAKES 4 LOAVES

5 g (¼ oz) fresh yeast

300 ml (½ pint) cold water

300 g (11 oz) strong bread flour

vegetable oil for the baking sheets

flaked salt, sesame seeds, sunflower
  seeds, pumpkin seeds or
  poppy seeds

DOUGH 2

15 g (½ oz) fresh yeast

300 ml (10 fl oz) cold water

1 batch of dough 1 (see above)

1 tablespoon salt

1 tablespoon caster sugar

420–480 g (14 ½ –16 ½ oz) bread flour

1. Crumble the yeast into a bowl and dissolve it in the water.
2. Add the flour and mix to make a smooth, soft dough.
3. Cover the bowl with clingfilm and leave the dough to prove for at least 4 hours at room temperature, or overnight in the refrigerator.
4. Preheat the oven to 240°C/475°F/gas 9.
5. Turn out the dough onto a floured surface and divide it into four. Gently press each portion into a rectangle.
6. Tuck in one of the long sides and roll up the dough. Shape the ends into points.
7. Twist the baguettes slightly and put them in a greased baguette tin or an ordinary baking sheet.
8. Leave the baguettes to prove under a tea towel for about 1 hour.
9. Brush the baguettes with water and sprinkle flaked salt and the seeds of your choice on top. Use a knife to make diagonal cuts in the surface of each loaf and immediately put the baking sheet in the centre of the oven.
10. Reduce the heat when the baguettes start to colour.
11. Bake for about 30 minutes. Leave to cool uncovered on a wire rack.

1. To make dough 2, crumble the yeast into a bowl and dissolve it in the water.
2. Add dough 1, the salt, sugar and flour and mix until the ingredients bind together. Knead the dough by hand or at a low speed in a mixer for about 15 minutes.
3. Cover the bowl with a tea towel and leave to prove for about 1 ½ hours. Proceed as above.

white toast bread

This is my favourite recipe for toast bread. It is easy to make and works perfectly for canapés as well as for toasting.

MAKES 2 LOAVES

50 g (2 oz) fresh yeast
500 ml (17 fl oz) tepid water
2 teaspoons honey
2 teaspoons golden syrup
100 ml (3 ½ fl oz) olive oil
1 ½ tablespoons flaked salt
120 g (4 ½ oz) durum wheat flour
600–660 g (about 1 ½ lb) strong bread
   flour
butter and sesame seeds or poppy
   seeds for the bread tins
flaked salt

1. Crumble the yeast into a bowl and add the water, honey, syrup, olive oil and flaked salt.
2. Add the flour and mix until the ingredients bind together and make a soft, elastic dough.
3. Cover the bowl with a tea towel and leave the dough to prove for about 40 minutes or until it has doubled in size.
4. Butter and coat two bread tins with sesame seeds or poppy seeds.
5. Divide the dough in half, knead and roll out into two loafs. Put the loaves in the bread tins.
6. Preheat the oven to 200°C/400°F/gas 6.
7. Cover the tins with a tea towel and leave the loaves to prove for about 30 minutes or until they have doubled in size.
8. Brush the loaves with water, sprinkle flaked salt on top and use a knife to score a lengthways depression down the centre of each loaf.
9. Bake immediately in the centre of the oven for 25–30 minutes and leave the loaves to cool on a wire rack.

fougasse from provence

Fougasse is a large, leaf-shaped, pull-apart bread from France. It can be flavoured with nuts, olives and fresh herbs. It tastes great and is perfect to eat just as it is.

MAKES 2 LOAVES

25 g (1 oz) fresh yeast
300 ml (½ pint) tepid water
100 ml (3 ½ fl oz) olive oil
5 sprigs of fresh rosemary
5 sprigs of fresh thyme
1 tablespoon flaked salt
30 g (1 ¼ oz) durum wheat flour
500 g (1 lb/2 oz) strong bread flour
65 g (2 ½ oz) pitted black olives
olive oil for brushing
flaked salt and fresh thyme

1. Crumble the yeast into a bowl and dissolve it with the water and the olive oil.
2. Chop the herbs finely and mix them with the liquid.
3. Add the flaked salt and the two flours and mix to form a soft, elastic dough. Work the dough in a mixer for about 15 minutes.
4. Cover the bowl with a tea towel and leave the dough to prove for about 1 hour or until it has doubled in size.
5. Divide the dough in two and knead half the chopped olives into each portion.
6. Roll out the dough into ovals about 1.5 cm (¾ in) thick. Put them on a baking sheet lined with greaseproof paper.
7. Cut 'veins' in the dough to resemble leaves and gently pull the dough to open up the cuts.
8. Preheat the oven to 250°C/500°F/gas 10.
9. Cover the bread with a tea towel and leave to prove for about 30 minutes or until it has doubled in size.
10. Brush the bread with olive oil, sprinkle flaked salt and fresh thyme on top and bake immediately in the centre of the oven for about 10 minutes or until golden. You will get a nice crust if you spray some water in the oven when you put in the bread.

homemade rosemary grissini

MAKES 30 GRISSINI

25 g (1 oz) fresh yeast (or use 3.5 g dry yeast, see page 218 for instructions)
150 ml (¼ pint) tepid water
1 teaspoon salt
2 teaspoons caster sugar
1 organic egg white
50 ml (2 fl oz) olive oil
2 sprigs of fresh rosemary
360 g (12 ½ oz) plain flour
flaked salt and chopped rosemary

1. Crumble the yeast into a bowl and stir in the water, salt and sugar.
2. Mix the egg white, olive oil and finely chopped rosemary into the liquid.
3. Add the flour a little at a time until the dough binds together.
4. Leave the dough to prove under a tea towel for about 1 ½ hours.
5. Preheat the oven to 175°C/350°F/gas 4.
6. Knead the dough on a floured surface and roll it into sticks, about the thickness of a pencil.
7. Brush the grissini with water, sprinkle with flaked salt and rosemary and bake in the centre of the oven for about 25 minutes or until they are golden brown.

french brioche

MAKES 20 BRIOCHES

25 g (1 oz) fresh yeast

5 organic eggs

420 g (15 oz) strong bread flour

1 teaspoon salt

60 g (2 ⅓ oz) caster sugar

375 g (13 oz) butter, softened

rape oil for the sealed plastic container

butter for the brioche tins

egg and salt for brushing

1. Crumble the yeast into a bowl, add the eggs and stir until the yeast has dissolved.
2. Mix together the dry ingredients and add them to the eggs.
3. Knead with dough hooks for about 15 minutes until it is smooth and elastic.
4. Divide the butter into four and add it gradually to the dough, mixing well between each addition.
5. Lightly oil a plastic container, pour in the dough and put on the lid. Leave the dough to prove in a warm place for about 2 hours or until it has doubled in size.
6. Knead the dough with your hands until it turns silky.
7. Return the dough to the plastic container and leave to rest in the refrigerator overnight.
8. Brush 20 small brioche tins with melted butter.
9. Roll out the dough and divide it into 20 even pieces. Put them in the tins.
10. Brush them with beaten egg mixed with salt. Be careful not to let the egg run between the dough and the tin or they will not rise.
11. Leave the dough to prove under a tea towel for about 1 hour until doubled in size.
12. Preheat the oven to 220°C/425°F/gas 7.
13. Cook in the centre of the oven for 8–10 minutes or until golden brown.

pain au chocolat

MAKES 8

250 g (9 oz) fresh puff pastry

100 g (4 oz) chocolate and hazelnut spread

25 g (1 oz) good quality dark chocolate (70% cocoa solids)

75 g (3 oz) homemade almond paste, see recipe page 208

zest of 1 orange

egg for brushing

slivered almonds

icing sugar

1. Preheat the oven to 175°C/350°F/gas 4.
2. Roll out the pastry on a lightly floured surface to a rectangle about 5 mm (¼ in) thick. Cut it into eight rectangles.
3. Spread a dab of chocolate spread over one short side of each rectangle.
4. Chop the chocolate coarsely and grate the almond paste. Mix with the orange zest and sprinkle over the chocolate spread.
5. Roll up the pieces from the short side and put them, seam down, on a baking sheet lined with greaseproof paper.
6. Brush with whisked egg and sprinkle with slivered almonds.
7. Bake in the centre of the oven for about 20 minutes or until golden.
8. Dust with icing sugar.

savoury bread

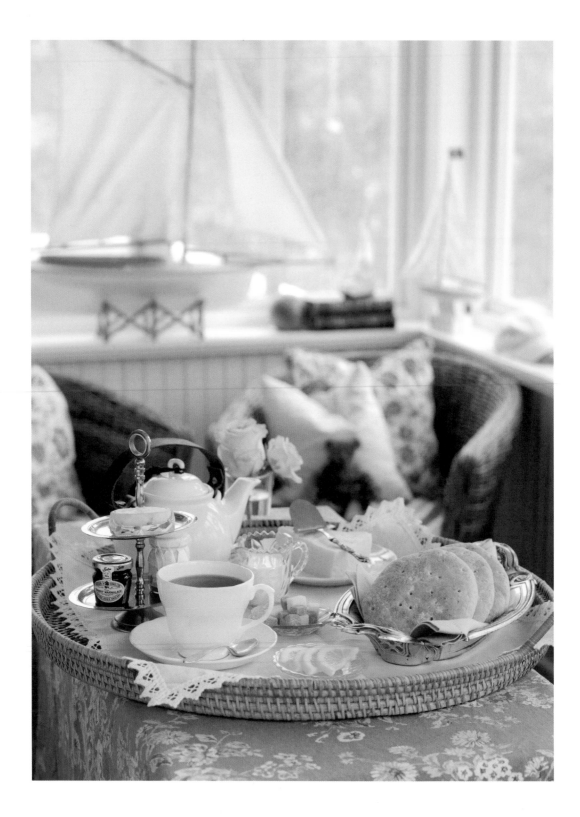

my sister's teacakes

When I was a little girl, my mother and I used to drink tea and munch juicy teacakes with cheese and marmalade. You can freeze teacakes it there are any left over, but it is best to freeze them when they are freshly baked.

MAKES 10

500 ml (17 fl oz) milk

165 g (5 ½ oz) rolled oats

½ tablespoon salt

1 tablespoon golden syrup

150 g (5 oz) unsalted butter

25 g (1 oz) fresh yeast

480–540 g (about 1 lb) strong bread flour

1. Heat the milk to about 50°C (120°F) and stir in the oats, salt and syrup. Leave to swell for about 20 minutes.
2. Melt the butter and stir into mixture.
3. Crumble the yeast into the mixture and mix thoroughly. Gradually add the flour, mixing to make a soft dough.
4. Cover the bowl with a tea towel and leave the dough to prove for about 30 minutes or until doubled in size.
5. Preheat the oven to 225°C/425°F/gas 7.
6. Knead the dough on a floured surface and form it into ten pieces, each about 1 cm (½ in) thick. Prick the tops with a fork and put them on a baking sheet lined with greaseproof paper. Leave to prove under a tea towel for about 30 minutes.
7. Bake in the centre of the oven for about 10 minutes.

soft flat bread

We often ate freshly baked soft flat breads when we were kids, and I've always had a special liking for them. Don't let them bake too long or the edges will turn hard.

MAKES 6

1 tablespoon fennel seeds

1 tablespoon aniseeds

2 teaspoons flaked salt

500 ml (17 fl oz) milk

45 g (1 ¾ oz) caster sugar

50 g (2 oz) fresh yeast

420 g (15 oz) strong bread flour

420 g (15 oz) sifted rye flour

100 g (4 oz) butter, softened

1. Pound the spices together with the salt in a mortar.
2. Heat the milk together with the spices and the sugar until tepid.
3. Crumble the yeast into a bowl and mix it with the liquid.
4. Add the flours a little at a time and work in a mixer to make a smooth, elastic dough. Add the butter and knead for about 10 minutes.
5. Cover the bowl with a tea towel and leave the dough to prove for about 1 hour or until doubled in size. Knock the dough back after about half an hour.
6. Turn the dough out on a floured surface and divide it into six. Roll each portion into a ball, then flatten them to about 1 cm (½ in) thick. Prick the tops with a fork and dust with flour.
7. Preheat the oven to 250°C/500°F/gas 10.
8. Put the breads on a baking sheet lined with greaseproof paper and leave to prove for about 40 minutes.
9. Bake in the centre of the oven for 7–8 minutes.

scones

This recipe is good enough for a royal tea party. You can vary the flavours endlessly. See the variations below and overleaf.

MAKES 6
BASIC RECIPE
450 g (1 lb) plain flour
½ teaspoon salt
1 ½ teaspoons baking powder
45 g (1 ¾ oz) demerara sugar
125 g (4 ½ oz) cold unsalted butter
1 organic egg
200 ml (7 fl oz) milk
egg, slivered almonds and demerara
   sugar for finishing

1. Preheat the oven to 230°C/450°F/gas 8.
2. Mix together the flour, salt, baking powder and sugar.
3. Dice the butter and mix it with the dry ingredients with your fingertips to make breadcrumbs.
4. Whisk the egg together with the milk.
5. Mix the liquid and dry ingredients together to make a stiff dough.
6. Turn out the dough on a lightly floured surface and roll it out to about 2.5 cm (1 in) thick. Use a biscuit cutter to cut out six rounds.
7. Put them on a baking sheet lined with greaseproof paper. Brush with beaten egg and sprinkle with slivered almonds and demerara sugar.
8. Bake in the centre of the oven for about 10 minutes or until golden.

blueberry & lemon scones

MAKES 6
1 batch of scone dough, see basic recipe
   above and instructions
60 g (2 ⅓ oz) plain flour
zest of 2 lemons
70 g (2 ⅔ oz) fresh or frozen
   blueberries
egg and demerara sugar for finishing

1. Prepare the dough according to the basic recipe, but add 60 g (2 ¼ oz) flour and lemon zest.
2. Carefully fold the blueberries into the dough, taking care that you do not crush them.
3. Follow the instructions in the basic recipe. Brush with beaten egg and sprinkle demerara sugar on top before putting the scones in the oven.

chocolate scones

MAKES 6
1 batch of scone dough, see basic recipe
   above and instructions
100 g (4 oz) good quality dark chocolate
   (70% cocoa solids)
egg and demerara sugar for finishing

1. Prepare the dough according to the basic recipe, but add coarsely chopped chocolate.
2. Follow the instructions in the basic recipe. Brush with beaten egg and sprinkle demerara sugar on top before putting the scones in the oven.

savoury bread

whole wheat scones

MAKES 6

1 batch of scone dough, see basic recipe
    page 176 and instructions
180 g (6 ¼ oz) whole wheat flour
    (instead of plain flour)
2 teaspoons cardamom pods
egg, poppy seeds and demerara sugar
    for finishing

1. Prepare the dough according to the basic recipe, but use whole wheat flour instead of the plain flour. Also bring the milk to the boil with the crushed cardamom pods before mixing the liquids with the dry ingredients.
2. Follow the instructions in the basic recipe. Brush with beaten egg and sprinkle poppy seeds and demerara sugar on top before putting the scones in the oven.

strawberry scones with walnuts

MAKES 6

1 batch of scone dough, see basic recipe
    page 176 and instructions
65 g (2 ½ oz) plain flour
150 g (5 oz) walnuts
70 g (2 ⅔ oz) fresh strawberries
egg and demerara sugar for finishing

1. Prepare the dough according to the basic recipe, but add an extra 65 g (2 ½ oz) flour with the coarsely chopped walnuts.
2. Hull and slice the strawberries. Fold them into the dough, taking care not to crush them.
3. Follow the instructions in the basic recipe. Brush with beaten egg and sprinkle demerara sugar on top before putting the scones in the oven.

coconut & lime scones

MAKES 6

1 batch of scone dough, see basic recipe
    page 176 and instructions
135 g (4 ¾ oz) desiccated coconut
zest of 2 limes
egg, desiccated coconut and demerara
    sugar for finishing

1. Toast the coconut in a dry saucepan.
2. Prepare the dough according to the basic recipe, but add the roasted coconut and the lime zest.
3. Follow the instructions in the basic recipe. Brush with beaten egg and sprinkle desiccated coconut and demerara sugar on top before putting the scones in the oven.

saffron scones

MAKES 6

1 batch of scone dough, see basic recipe
    page 176 and instructions
1 pinch of saffron
egg, slivered almonds and demerara
    sugar for finishing

1. Prepare the dough according to the basic recipe, but bring the milk to the boil together with the saffron before mixing the liquids with the dry ingredients.
2. Follow the instructions in the basic recipe. Brush with beaten egg and sprinkle slivered almonds and demerara sugar on top before putting the scones in the oven.

spicy raisin scones

MAKES 6

1 batch of scone dough, see basic recipe
    page 176 and instructions
1 teaspoon ground clove
2 teaspoons ground cinnamon
120 g (4 ½ oz) currants
egg, pumpkin seeds and demerara
    sugar for finishing

1. Prepare the dough according to the basic recipe, but bring the milk to the boil together with the spices and the currants before mixing the liquids with the dry ingredients.
2. Follow the instructions in the basic recipe. Brush with beaten egg and sprinkle pumpkin seeds and demerara sugar on top before putting the scones in the oven.

muesli scones with sunflower seeds

MAKES 6

1 batch of scone dough, see basic recipe
    page 176 and instructions
90 g (3 ½) fruit muesli (instead of
    50 g/2 oz plain flour)
egg, sunflower seeds and demerara
    sugar for finishing

1. Prepare the dough according to the basic recipe, but replace 50 g (2 oz) of the flour with 90 g (3 ⅓ oz) fruit muesli.
2. Follow the instructions in the basic recipe. Brush with beaten egg and sprinkle sunflower seeds and demerara sugar on top before putting the scones in the oven.

stilton scones with dried fruits

MAKES 6

1 batch of scone dough, see basic recipe
    page 176 and instructions
100 g (4 oz) blue cheese, preferably
    Stilton
100 g (4 oz) walnuts
75 g (3 oz) dried apricots
75 g (3 oz) dried figs
egg and demerara sugar for finishing

1. Prepare the dough according to the basic recipe, but add the crumbled blue cheese and coarsely chopped walnuts, apricots and figs.
2. Follow the instructions in the basic recipe. Brush with beaten egg and sprinkle demerara sugar on top before putting the scones in the oven.

hearty wholemeal & crisp bread

I love to serve a sweet, dark bread with dried fruit and nuts when I am putting together a cheese platter. The sweetness of the fruit and the saltiness of the cheese are a great combination. The quick and simple French spicy bread *pain d'épices* is my first choice as a complement to dessert cheeses, while the fruit bread, which is baked from sourdough, goes well with milder cheeses for an open sandwich. When it comes to rye breads, I have many favourites, but there are few things that beat a warm rye roll with some cheese and marmalade.

pain d'épices

Pain d'épices is an outstanding bread for the cheese board. It is really quick and easy to make. Just mix the ingredients together and bake it.

MAKES 1 LOAF
100 ml (3 ½ fl oz) honey
45 g (1 ¾ oz) demerara sugar
150 ml (¼ pint) whipping cream
1 teaspoon aniseeds
1 teaspoon caraway seeds
1 teaspoon coriander seeds
1 teaspoon fennel seeds
1 teaspoon ground ginger
1 teaspoon ground cinnamon
80 g (3 ½ oz) dried apricots
65 g (2 ½ oz) pumpkin seeds
40 g (1 ½ oz) walnuts
125 g (4 ½ oz) plain flour
1 teaspoon flaked salt
2 teaspoons baking soda
butter and slivered almonds for the tin

1. Preheat the oven to 150°C/300°F/gas 2.
2. Bring the honey, demerara sugar, whipping cream and the spices to the boil in a saucepan. Pour into a bowl and leave to cool.
3. Chop the apricots and mix them with the pumpkin seeds and walnuts. Add the flour, salt and baking soda.
4. Mix the dry ingredients with the liquids.
5. Butter and coat a 23 cm (9 in) sponge tin with crushed slivered almonds. Pour the mixture into the tin. Bake in the centre of the oven for 40–50 minutes or until a skewer inserted into the centre comes out clean.

classic crisp bread

My mother-in-law loves this crisp bread; it's her absolute favourite. She always selects organic products and loves wholemeal bread. This is not the coarsest kind, but it is really good and it doesn't have to prove because it uses baking soda in the dough.

MAKES 20 CRISP BREADS
500 ml (17 fl oz) buttermilk
150 ml (¼ pint) golden syrup
2 teaspoons fennel seeds
2 teaspoons aniseeds
900 g (2 lb) sifted rye flour
2 teaspoons salt
2 teaspoons baking soda

1. Mix the buttermilk with the syrup.
2. Pound the fennel seeds and the aniseeds in a mortar.
3. Mix together all the dry ingredients, add the liquid and knead into a dough.
4. Divide the dough into 20 pieces, roll them out into round cakes and prick them with a fork.
5. Fry the cakes for about a minute on each side in a dry frying pan over a medium heat. Leave to cool on a wire rack.

Using sourdough improves the bread's texture and taste and makes it keep longer. A sourdough is made from only water and flour, and when it is left at room temperature for a while it will start producing lactic and acetic acids and a natural yeast culture. If it's looked after properly, a sourdough came become very old and I've heard of sourdoughs in Finland where they've been passed down for generations! Baking with normal yeast and sourdough at the same time is an easy and good way to start experimenting with sourdough bread at home. It might sound complicated to use sourdough but it really isn't and the result is much more satisfying than bread made with yeast alone.

sourdough

Sometimes conventional flour is too 'clean' to make a good sourdough. Organic flour isn't as refined and is better. As long as you keep the sourdough in the refrigerator it will rest. The day before you want to use it, feed it with some rye flour and water to 'wake it'.

MAKES 1 BATCH OF RYE SOURDOUGH
400 ml (14 fl oz) tepid water
270 g (9 ½ oz) organic wholemeal rye flour

MAKES 1 BATCH OF WHEAT SOURDOUGH
400 ml (14 fl oz) tepid water
270 g (9 ½ oz) organic plain flour

1. Mix 200 ml (7 fl oz) water with 150 g (5 oz) flour. Cover with clingfilm and leave at room temperature for two days.
2. Add 100 ml (3 ½ fl oz) water and 65 g (2 ½ oz) flour. Mix carefully. Cover with clingfilm and leave at room temperature for another day.
3. Add another 100 ml (3 ½ fl oz) water and 65 g (2 ½ oz) flour. Mix, cover with clingfilm and leave at room temperature for one more day.

fruit & hazelnut sourdough

MAKES 2 LOAVES
25 g (1 oz) fresh yeast
400 ml (14 fl oz) cold water
1 tablespoon dark treacle
2 teaspoons salt
2 teaspoons ground cinnamon
100 g (4 oz) rye sourdough (optional), see basic recipe above
230 g (8 ½ oz) wholemeal rye flour
420 g (15 oz) bread flour
150 g (5 oz) hazelnuts
100 g (4 oz) raisins
1 bag of mixed dried fruits
wholemeal rye flour for baking
butter for the tins

1. Crumble the yeast in a bowl and add the water, treacle, salt and cinnamon.
2. Add the sourdough (if using), rye flour and some plain flour a little at a time and knead slowly in a food processor until the dough is elastic.
3. Work the dough for about 5 minutes at a higher speed and add the whole hazelnuts, raisins and coarsely chopped dried fruits.
4. Leave the dough to prove under a tea towel for about 1 hour or until doubled in size.
5. Put an empty roasting tin at the bottom of the oven and preheat the oven to 240°C/475°F/gas 9.
6. Divide the dough in two. Fold the dough a couple of times and shape loaves. Roll the loaves in wholemeal rye flour and put in two buttered rectangular loaf tins. Leave to prove under a tea towel for about 1 hour.
7. Using a sharp knife, carefully score three cuts lengthways before putting the loaves in the oven. Pour ¾ coffee cup water in the hot roasting pan and close the oven door quickly. Lower the heat to 230°C/450°F/gas 8 and bake the bread for about 30 minutes.
8. Lift the bread out of the tins and leave to cool on a wire rack.

danish rye bread

This bread is even better if you leave it for a day before eating it. It's very juicy and lasts well: it will keep in a plastic bag for 1–2 weeks.

MAKES 3 LOAVES

STARTER

2 tablespoons fennel seeds

2 tablespoons aniseeds

2 tablespoons ground caraway seeds

2 tablespoons salt

500 ml (17 fl oz) boiling water

340 g (11 ¾ oz) rye grits

65 g (2 ½ oz) linseeds

DOUGH

90 g (3 ½ oz) fresh yeast

500 ml (17 fl oz) tepid water

250 ml (8 fl oz) dark treacle

240 g (8 ½ oz) sunflower seeds

65 g (2 ½ oz) pumpkin seeds

585 g (1 ¼ lb) wholemeal rye flour

420 g (15 oz) bread flour

1. Grind the fennel seeds and aniseeds in a mortar. Mix all the ingredients for the starter in a bowl. Cover with clingfilm and leave at room temperature for 1–3 days.
2. Crumble the yeast into a bowl. Add the water and the treacle.
3. Stir the starter into the bowl.
4. Blend in the sunflower seeds, pumpkin seeds and add the flour a little at a time. The dough should be very sticky.
5. Knead with dough hooks in a food processor for about 30 minutes. The dough should still be sticky.
6. Preheat the oven to 240°C/475°F/gas 9.
7. Line rectangular bread tins with greaseproof paper and fill with the dough. Sprinkle some rye flour on top and leave the bread to prove for about 30 minutes.
8. Use a knife to make lengthways cuts in the top of each loaf and bake in the lower part of the oven for about 1 ½ hours. Use a vaporiser to spray water into the oven during the baking (once or twice) to give the bread a good crust.
9. Cover the bread with foil after about 30 minutes to prevent the loaves from turning too dark.
10. Remove the bread from the tins and leave to cool on a wire rack.

sporty brown rolls

Use a measuring cup for measuring the flour for these healthy rolls. Pour the flour into the measuring cup until you reach the required weight. If you scoop the flour from the bag with a small measuring spoon the flour might become too tightly packed and you will end up with more flour than is necessary for the dough.

MAKES 30 SMALL ROLLS

STARTER

500 ml (17 fl oz) boiling water

2 ½ teaspoons aniseeds

2 ½ teaspoons caraway seeds

2 ½ teaspoons coriander seeds

2 ½ teaspoons fennel seeds

2 tablespoons salt

170 g (6 oz) rye grits

130 g (4 ¾ oz) crushed linseeds

120 g (4 ½ oz) rye flour

170 g (6 oz) whole boiled spelt

DOUGH

500 ml (17 fl oz) milk

50 g (2 oz) fresh yeast

200 ml (7 fl oz) dark treacle

180 g (6 ¼ oz) hazelnuts

120 g (4 ½ oz) high-fibre rolled oats

75 g (3 oz) raisins

80 g (3 ⅓ oz) dried apricots

80 g (3 ⅓ oz) dried figs

150 g (5 oz) rye flour

240 g (8 ½ oz) plain spelt flour

330 g (12 oz) bread flour

sunflower seeds

1. Mix all the ingredients for the starter in a bowl. Cover with clingfilm and leave the mixture to swell at room temperature for at least 30 minutes.
2. Heat the milk to tepid, 38°C (100°F).
3. Crumble the yeast into a bowl and stir in the milk.
4. Add the starter to the bowl and stir to combine.
5. Blend in the treacle, hazelnuts, rolled oats, raisins, chopped apricots and chopped figs.
6. Add the flour a little at a time. The dough should be really sticky.
7. Drop the buns onto a baking sheet lined with greaseproof paper and sprinkle sunflower seeds and flour on top.
8. Preheat the oven to 200°C/400°F/gas 6.
9. Leave the buns to prove under a tea towel for about 1 ½ hours.
10. Bake in the centre of the oven for about 20 minutes.

morning glory rolls

These rolls are perfect at breakfast time. Eat them freshly baked with butter and Cheddar cheese.

MAKES 14 ROLLS

35 g (1 ¼ oz) fresh yeast

1 teaspoon caraway seeds

1 teaspoon aniseeds

50 g (2 oz) butter

2 tablespoons honey

300 ml (½ pint) cold water

65 g (2 ½ oz) sunflower seeds

65 g (2 ½ oz) pumpkin seeds

2 teaspoons flaked salt

65 g (2 ½ oz) wholemeal spelt flour

65 g (2 ½ oz) wholemeal flour

120 g (4 ½ oz) plain spelt flour

240–360 g (8 ½–12 ½ oz) bread flour

egg for brushing

flaked salt, sunflower seeds and
    pumpkin seeds

1. Crumble the yeast into a bowl.
2. Pound the caraway seeds and the aniseeds in a mortar.
3. Melt together the butter, spices and honey. Remove from the heat and add the water. Pour the liquid over the yeast.
4. Toast the sunflower and pumpkin seeds with the flaked salt in a dry saucepan. Add the liquid and stir.
5. Mix in the flour a little at a time and work the dough until it starts to come away from the sides of the bowl. It should be a bit sticky.
6. Work the dough slowly in a food processor for about 20 minutes.
7. Cover with a tea towel and leave to prove for about 45 minutes or until doubled in size.
8. Preheat the oven to 200°C/400°F/gas 6.
9. Turn out the dough onto a floured surface and divide it into 14 pieces. Transfer the rolls to a baking sheet lined with greaseproof paper and leave to prove for about 1 hour.
10. Brush the buns with beaten egg, sprinkle flaked salt, sunflower seeds and pumpkin seeds on top.
11. Bake in the centre of the oven for about 10 minutes.

sweet rye & raisin rolls

If you use stone-ground flour you need to add more water than if you are using conventional flour. Organic stone-ground flour gives the buns a richer taste.

MAKES 12 ROLLS

35 g (1 ¼ oz) butter

300 ml (½ pint) milk

50 ml (2 fl oz) dark treacle

1 teaspoon salt

1 teaspoon aniseeds

1 teaspoon caraway seeds

1 teaspoon coriander seeds

1 teaspoon fennel seeds

50 g (2 oz) fresh yeast

65 g (2 ½ oz) raisins

200 g (7 oz) rye flour

280 g (10 oz) strong bread flour

1. Melt the butter and add the milk, treacle, salt and seeds.
2. Warm the liquid to tepid, 38°C (100°F).
3. Crumble the yeast into a bowl and dissolve it in the liquid.
4. Stir in the raisins and some of the flours a little at a time to give a smooth dough.
5. Cover the bowl with a tea towel and leave the dough to prove for about 30 minutes or until doubled in size.
6. Preheat the oven to 225°C/425°F/gas 7.
7. Divide the dough into 12 pieces and dip them in sifted rye flour. Put them on a baking sheet lined with greaseproof paper, and leave to prove for about 30 minutes.
8. Bake in the centre of the oven for about 10 minutes.

honey & buttermilk bread

I invented this wonderful bread one day in a summer cottage. It's definitely a family favourite.

MAKES 2 LOAVES

50 g (2 oz) butter

500 ml (17 fl oz) buttermilk

50 g (2 oz) fresh yeast (or use 7 g dry yeast, see page 218 for instructions)

200 ml (7 fl oz) dark treacle

2 teaspoons salt

500–550 g (18–20 oz) strong bread flour

150 g (5 oz) rye flour

1. Melt the butter and mix with the buttermilk. Warm until tepid, 38°C (100°F).
2. Crumble the yeast in a bowl and add the liquid, treacle and salt.
3. Add the bread flour and rye flour a little at a time until the dough binds together and becomes soft and elastic. Knead in the last of the flour by hand.
4. Cover the bowl with a tea towel and leave the dough to prove until doubled in size.
5. Preheat the oven to 200°C/400°F/gas 6.
6. Knead and shape the dough into two loaves and put them in floured bread tins or on a baking sheet lined with greaseproof paper. Cover with a tea towel and leave to prove for about 40 minutes.
7. Bake in the centre of the oven for 35–40 minutes. Cover with foil after 20 minutes to prevent the bread from over-browning.

aunt sally's cranberry & raisin bread

When I was a child, we often baked this juicy wholemeal cranberry bread. We all loved it, and it's still one of my favourites.

MAKES 2 LOAVES

400 ml (14 fl oz) warm water

200 ml (7 fl oz) cranberry jam

100 ml (3 ½ fl oz) olive oil

50 ml (2 fl oz) golden syrup

1 teaspoon vinegar

1 tablespoon salt

1 tablespoon caraway seeds

1 tablespoon fennel seeds

140 g (4 ¾ oz) raisins

65 g (2 ½ oz) linseeds

12 g (½ oz) dry yeast

130 g (4 ¾ oz) wholemeal flour

120 g (4 ½ oz) rye flour

600–660 g (about 1 ¼ lb) strong bread flour

1. Mix the warm water, about 40°C (105°F), cranberry jam, olive oil, syrup, vinegar, salt and spices pounded in a mortar, raisins and linseeds in a bowl.
2. Mix the dry yeast with the wholemeal flour, the rye flour and the bread flour. Stir into the liquid a little at a time until the dough binds together. It should be sticky.
3. Cover with a tea towel and leave to prove for about 1 hour or until doubled in size.
4. Knead and shape into two loaves and put them on a baking sheet lined with greaseproof paper or in greased rectangular bread tins.
5. Preheat the oven to 175°C/350°F/gas 4.
6. Cover with a tea towel and leave to prove for about 1 ½ hours.
7. Bake in the centre of the oven for about 40 minutes or until golden.

delicious rye rolls

This was one of the first recipes I learned during my time in the restaurant business. It has always been one of my favourites.

MAKES 4 ROLL CAKES
50 g (2 oz) butter
50 ml (2 fl oz) olive oil
400 ml (14 fl oz) milk
100 ml (3 ½ fl oz) dark treacle
2 teaspoons salt
1 teaspoon aniseeds
1 teaspoon caraway seeds
1 teaspoon coriander seeds
1 teaspoon fennel seeds
12 g (½ oz) dry yeast
150 g (5 oz) rye flour
1 teaspoon vinegar
500-550 g (18-20 oz) strong bread flour

1. Melt the butter in a saucepan. Add the olive oil, milk, syrup, salt and seeds and heat to about 45°C (115°F).
2. Mix the dry yeast and rye flour in a bowl and pour in the liquid. Add vinegar and knead.
3. Add the bread flour a little at a time and mix until the dough starts to come away from the sides of the bowl.
4. Cover with a tea towel and leave to prove for about 1 hour or until doubled in size.
5. Turn out the dough onto a floured surface. Knead and shape into four round cakes and score a cross on top of each one.
6. Put them on a baking sheet lined with greaseproof paper and prick with a fork.
7. Preheat the oven to 200°C/400°F/gas 6.
8. Cover with a tea towel and prove for about 30 minutes.
9. Bake in the centre of the oven for about 15 minutes.

potato flatbread

MAKES 20 FLATBREADS
15 g (½ oz) fresh yeast
1 teaspoon aniseeds
1 teaspoon fennel seeds
1 ½ teaspoon salt
50 g (2 oz) butter
250 ml (8 fl oz) milk
2 tablespoons golden syrup
2 tablespoons caster sugar
75 g (3 oz) rye flour
250 g (9 oz) strong bread flour

FILLING
300 g (11 oz) warm, freshly boiled peeled potatoes
90 g (3 ½ oz) sifted rye flour (see above)
90 g (3 ½ oz) strong bread flour

1. Crumble the yeast into a bowl.
2. Crush the seeds together with the salt in a mortar.
3. Melt the butter and heat it with the milk, syrup, caster sugar and crushed seeds until tepid, 38°C (100°F).
4. Pour the liquid over the yeast and stir thoroughly.
5. Add the flour a little at a time and stir to make a sticky dough.
6. Cover with a tea towel and leave to prove for about 1 hour or until doubled in size.
7. Mash the boiled potatoes with a fork and knead them into the dough. Add the rye flour and bread flour and mix to make a smooth dough.
8. Divide into 20 pieces and roll into thin round cakes. Prick them with a fork.
9. Fry the cakes for about a minute on each side until they get a little colour in a dry frying pan at medium heat. Be careful not to fry too long or the cakes will turn hard.

traditional swedish crisp bread

I often bake these crisp breads for the cheeseboard and for midsummer parties. They should be really brittle and crisp, so roll the dough as thinly as possible.

MAKES 24 CRISP BREADS
500 ml (17 fl oz) milk
½ tablespoon honey
½ tablespoon golden syrup
1 teaspoon salt
1 teaspoon fennel seeds
1 teaspoon caraway seeds
10 g (¼ oz) fresh yeast
120 g (4 ½ oz) plain flour
180 g (6 ¼ oz) rye flour
450 g (1 lb) wholemeal flour

1. Heat the milk with the honey, syrup, salt and ground seeds, until tepid, 38°C (100°F).
2. Crumble the yeast into a bowl and dissolve it in the liquid.
3. Add the flour a little at a time and work into an elastic dough.
4. Preheat the oven to 220°C/425°F/gas 7.
5. Cover with a tea towel and leave to prove for about 1 hour.
6. Turn the dough out on a lightly floured surface and roll out thinly. Cut out about 24 breads and put them on baking sheets lined with greaseproof paper.
7. Bake in the centre of the oven for 3–4 minutes or until the breads begin to colour, turn them over and bake for another minute.

vanilla & poppy seed crisp bread

Brush the bread with beaten egg and sprinkle poppy seeds and black pepper on top. Sometimes I use other seeds, like pumpkin seeds or sesame seeds. It's a perfect snack to enjoy with a drink.

MAKES 30 CRISP BREADS
1 vanilla pod
150 ml (¼ pint) water
1 teaspoon honey
1 teaspoon salt
15 g (½ oz) fresh yeast
2 tablespoons poppy seeds
1 tablespoon olive oil
120 g (4 ½ oz) plain flour
65 g (2 ½ oz) wholemeal rye flour

1. Halve the vanilla pod lengthways and scrape out the seeds. Bring the water, vanilla seeds, honey and salt to the boil.
2. Leave to cool until tepid, 38°C (100°F). Strain out the vanilla seeds.
3. Crumble the yeast in a bowl and dissolve it in the liquid.
4. Add the poppy seeds and olive oil.
5. Add the flour a little at a time and work into an elastic dough.
6. Preheat the oven to 200°C/400°F/gas 6.
7. Cover with a tea towel and leave to prove for about 1 hour.
8. Turn the dough out on a lightly floured surface and roll it out thinly. Cut out about 30 breads and put them on a baking sheets lined with greaseproof paper.
9. Bake in the centre of the oven for 3–4 minutes until the breads begin to colour, turn them over and bake for another minute.

turbo fast buttermilk bread

This really quick and healthy bread is a favourite with all my friends. I vary this recipe, sometimes adding nuts, like almonds, walnuts or pecan nuts. At other times I make it with dried fruit. You can't find an easier bread made with baking powder.

MAKES 1 LOAF

450 ml (¾ pint) buttermilk

100 ml (3 ½ fl oz) dark treacle

80 g (3 ⅓ oz) dried apricots or figs

65 g (2 ½ oz) hazelnuts

75 g (3 oz) raisins

85 g (3 ¼ oz) rye grits

40 g (1 ½ oz) rolled oats

165 g (5 ½ oz) wholemeal rye flour

180 g (6 ¼ oz) plain flour

65 g (2 ½ oz) crushed linseeds

65 g (2 ½ oz) sunflower seeds

1 ½ teaspoons salt

1 ½ teaspoons baking powder

1 ½ teaspoons bicarbonate soda

½ teaspoon aniseeds

½ teaspoon caraway seeds

½ teaspoon coriander seeds

½ teaspoon fennel seeds

rolled oats

1. Preheat the oven to 200°C/400°F/gas 6.
2. Mix the buttermilk and the syrup in a bowl.
3. Chop the fruit and the hazelnuts really coarsely, mix with the raisins and the dry ingredients. Stir into the buttermilk.
4. Line a loaf tin with greaseproof paper, leaving the excess paper to overlap at the ends and sides.
5. Pour the mixture into the tin, sprinkle some rolled oats on top and bake in the centre of the oven for about 45 minutes.

baking without an oven

Sometimes I get a strong urge to bake something only to realise that I do not have an oven to hand! I may be on holiday somewhere or perhaps my own oven has finally given up the ghost. This is a great opportunity to choose one of the following recipes that rely on cold rather than heat to finish them off.

chocolate marzipan log

This was originally a way of using up dry cakes in the baker's shop. They usually mix both sponge crumbs and cake crumbs together, and I think this is a wonderful way of using a sponge that has gone dry.

MAKES 18 SMALL LOGS
50 g (2 oz) unsalted butter, softened
150 g (5 oz) crumbs from a sponge or from biscuits
2 teaspoons good quality cocoa powder
arrack liqueur or your favourite tipple for flavour
300 g (11 oz) green marzipan and green
    food colouring
icing sugar for rolling
100 g (4 oz) good quality dark chocolate
    (70% cocoa solids)

1. Mix together the butter and the crumbs until creamy and stir in cocoa powder.
2. Add the liqueur of your choice.
3. Divide the dough into three pieces and roll them into long sausages. Put them in the freezer.
4. Divide the marzipan into three and shape into sausages then roll out as thinly as possible. If the marzipan becomes sticky, dust it with icing sugar.
5. Take the dough out of the freezer and roll the marzipan around them. Make sure the joins overlap and are underneath the biscuits. Put the biscuits back into the freezer.
6. Melt one-third of the chocolate in a bowl set over a pan of simmering water. Remove the bowl from the pan as soon as the chocolate has melted.
7. Chop and add the remaining chocolate. Stir until it has melted. Leave to cool.
8. Take the rolls out of the freezer and cut them into 5 cm (2 in) pieces. Dip the ends in the chocolate. Store the logs in the refrigerator.

cognac bomb

MAKES 20
100 g (4 oz) unsalted butter, softened
135 g (4 3/4 oz) caster sugar
120 g (4 1/2 oz) rolled oats
3 tablespoons good quality cocoa powder
2 tablespoons cold coffee
arrack liqueur or cognac
chocolate sprinkles

1. Mix together the butter, sugar and rolled oats in a bowl.
2. Stir in the cocoa powder and then the cold coffee.
3. Stir in the liqueur or cognac.
4. Shape into balls and roll in chocolate sprinkles. Store in the refrigerator.

lion bars

MAKES 20 BARS
300 g (11 oz) crunchy peanut butter
200 ml (7 fl oz) golden syrup
90 g (3 1/2 oz) caster sugar
1 tablespoon vanilla sugar
135 g (4 3/4 oz) desiccated coconut
55 g (2 1/4 oz) Rice Krispies
250 g (9 oz) good quality dark chocolate
    (70% cocoa solids)

1. Melt the peanut butter, syrup, sugar and vanilla sugar over a low heat.
2. Toast the desiccated coconut in a dry frying pan.
3. Stir in the coconut and Rice Krispies into the mixture.
4. Divide the mixture into two rectangular loaf tins lined with clingfilm.
5. Leave to set in the refrigerator for about 1 1/2 hours.
6. Melt the chocolate in a bowl set over a pan of simmering water. Cut the cake into 1.5 cm (3/4 in) bars and dip into the melted chocolate.
7. Put back into the refrigerator and leave to set for a few hours.

chocolate radio cake

The heyday of the radio cake was in the 1930s and 1940s when the radio was in fashion. The story goes that the cake got its name because it resembles the loudspeaker of an old-fashioned radio.

MAKES 1 CAKE

200 ml (7 fl oz) whipping cream
100 ml (3 ½ fl oz) milk
2 tablespoons honey
300 g (11 oz) good quality dark chocolate
    (70% cocoa solids)
15 g (½ oz) unsalted butter
100 g (4 oz) finger biscuits

1. Bring the cream, milk and honey to the boil.
2. Remove the saucepan from the heat and add the finely chopped chocolate. Stir until the chocolate melts. Add the butter bit by bit.
3. Line a loaf tin with clingfilm. Pour in a thin layer of the mixture. Add a layer of biscuits.
4. Continue layering the mixture and biscuits, ending with mixture. Leave in the refrigerator overnight.
5. Turn the cake out of the tin and cut into slices while it's still cold.

chocolate coconut bomb

MAKES 15

100 g (4 oz) unsalted butter, softened
135 g (4 ¾ oz) caster sugar
120 g (4 ½ oz) rolled oats
1 teaspoon vanilla sugar
3 tablespoons good quality cocoa powder
2 tablespoons cold coffee
desiccated coconut

1. Mix together the butter, sugar and the rolled oats in a bowl.
2. Stir in the vanilla sugar and the cocoa powder. Add the coffee.
3. Shape into balls and roll in desiccated coconut. Store in the refrigerator.

mint crisp

MAKES 15 PIECES

300 g (11 oz) good quality dark chocolate
    (70% cocoa solids)
a few drops peppermint flavouring
75 g (3 oz) bran flakes
100 g (4 oz) homemade almond paste, see recipe
    page 208

1. Melt one-third of the chocolate in a bowl set over a pan of simmering water. Chop the remaining chocolate finely.
2. Remove the melted chocolate from the heat and stir in the chopped chocolate. Add a few drops of peppermint flavouring.
3. Leave the chocolate to cool completely. Stir occasionally until it starts to thicken and you can see marks from the spoon.
4. Blend in the bran flakes and grated almond paste. Stir just enough to cover the bran flakes evenly.
5. Drop the mixture in small peaks onto a sheet of greaseproof paper and leave to set in the refrigerator.

rocky road

These really are the best sweets in the world.

MAKES 20 PIECES

600 g (1 lb/5 oz) good quality dark chocolate
    (70% cocoa solids)
2 bags toffees
2 handfuls of mini marshmallows
210 g (7 ½ oz) salted peanuts
65 g (2 ½ oz) peeled pistachios

1. Melt the chocolate in a bowl set over a pan of simmering water. Leave to cool a little.
2. Chop the toffees and mix all the ingredients with the melted chocolate.
3. Pour the mixture into a square baking tin lined with greaseproof paper to a depth of 2.5 cm (1 in). Leave to set in the refrigerator, then cut into squares.

chocolate truffles

This basic truffle recipe can be varied with all kinds of delicious flavourings. You can use chilli and ground cinnamon, lemon zest, peppermint flavouring, dark rum, whisky, ground ginger or crushed cardamom. Alternatively, roll the truffles in different kinds of flavoured sugar. I use demerara sugar mixed with crushed cardamom or ground cinnamon. It's also really nice to mix caster sugar with lemon or orange zest (but let the mix dry first).

MAKES 20

250 g (9 oz) good quality dark chocolate (70% cocoa solids)
150 ml (¼ pint) whipping cream
2 tablespoons honey
15 g (½ oz) unsalted butter
1 pinch flaked salt
cocoa powder

1. Finely chop the the chocolate.
2. Bring the whipping cream and honey to the boil and pour the mixture over the chocolate stirring continually. Add the butter and the flaked salt and mix thoroughly.
3. Pour the chocolate into a plastic food container with a lid and leave to set in the refrigerator for about 4 hours.
4. Shape the chocolate into balls (truffles) and roll them in cocoa powder.

chocolate chip muesli bar

MAKES 20

250 g (9 oz) dried figs
1 tablespoon good quality cocoa powder
1 tablespoon warm espresso coffee
200 g (7 oz) yellow raisins
185 g (6 ½ oz) muesli with dried fruits
15 g (½ oz) cornflakes
200 g (7 oz) good quality dark chocolate (70% cocoa solids)

1. Cut the stems off the figs and chop them coarsely.
2. Mix them in a blender together with the cocoa powder and coffee.
3. Add half of the raisins and the muesli. Process for a few seconds to make a paste.
4. Transfer the paste to a bowl and pour in the remaining raisins, muesli and cornflakes.
5. Chop the chocolate and mix half of it into the paste.
6. Roll out the paste between two sheets of greaseproof paper until it is 1 cm (½ in) thick.
7. Melt the remaining chocolate in a bowl set over a pan of simmering water. Brush the cake with the chocolate.
8. Leave to set in the refrigerator. Cut the cake into pieces when the chocolate has set.

sauces, creams & marmalades

It's what's on the inside that counts. Many of our cakes would not reach their true glory without their beautiful and tasty fillings. Vanilla cream, elderflower cream and lemon curd are a few of the key performers on my baking stage. In this chapter you will find some of my favourite marmalade and jam recipes together with other indispensible accessories for buns, pies and desserts. Pick and choose your favourites from these lovely recipes.

speedy vanilla custard

SERVES 4

½ vanilla pod
3 organic egg yolks
45 g (1 ¾ oz) caster sugar
300 ml (½ pint) whipping cream

1. Split the vanilla pod lengthways and scrape out the seeds.
2. Beat together the egg yolks, sugar and vanilla seeds until pale and creamy.
3. Whip the cream until it is softly peaking and blend it into the egg mixture.

exotic mango sauce

SERVES 4

1 large ripe mango
90 g (3 ½ oz) caster sugar
150 ml (¼ pint) water
1 tablespoon light rum
zest and juice of 1 lime

1. Peel the mango, remove the stone and cut the flesh into pieces.
2. Boil the mango with the sugar and water for about 5 minutes.
3. Flavour with the rum and lime zest and juice.
4. Use a hand-held mixer to blend the sauce until smooth.
5. Strain the sauce through a fine sieve and leave to cool.

homemade almond paste

MAKES 500 G (1 ¼ LB)

250 g (9 oz) almonds
225 g (8 oz) caster sugar

1. Blanch the almonds.
2. Process the almonds in a blender to a fine powder.
3. Add the sugar and mix for 5–7 minutes to make a smooth paste.

forest berry sauce

SERVES 4

180 g (6 ¼ oz) fresh or frozen strawberries or blueberries
90 g (3 ½ oz) caster sugar
150 ml (¼ pint) water
juice of 1 lemon

1. In a stainless steel saucepan bring the berries, sugar, water and lemon juice to the boil and simmer for about 5 minutes.
2. Mix until smooth using a hand blender.
3. Strain the sauce through a fine sieve. Leave to cool.

crème patisserie

The most difficult part of making crème patisserie is simmering to thicken. It is important to beat the mixture continually during this process. As soon as the custard has thickened you have to pour it into a cold bowl. Never put your fingers in it because it separates easily.

MAKES ENOUGH FOR 1 CAKE

1 vanilla pod
500 ml (17 fl oz) milk
135 g (4 ¾ oz) caster sugar
7 organic egg yolks
75 g (3 oz) cornflour
50 g (2 oz) unsalted butter, softened

1. Halve the vanilla pod lengthways and scrape out the seeds. Bring the milk and vanilla seeds to the boil in a saucepan. Strain out the vanilla seeds.
2. Beat together the eggs, sugar and cornflour until pale and fluffy in a bowl.
3. Pour the hot milk into the egg mixture, beating continuously.
4. Pour the mixture back into the saucepan and heat, beating all the time. Pour into a cold bowl when it has thickened substantially.
5. Melt the butter and add it to the custard, beating until it is completely incorporated.
6. Transfer to the refrigerator.

lime curd

MAKES 1 SMALL JAR

6 limes

135 g (4 ¾ oz) caster sugar

50 g (2 oz) butter

2 tablespoons cornflour

2 organic eggs

2 organic egg yolks

1. Mix the zest and juice of four limes.
2. Bring the lime juice, zest, sugar and butter to the boil.
3. Strain the liquid.
4. Blend the cornflour with the juice from remaining limes. Stir into the warm liquid.
5. Beat the eggs and stir into the liquid. Return the saucepan to the heat and simmer, stirring constantly, until the curd thickens.
6. Pour into a clean jar or bowl and leave to cool.

lemon curd

MAKES 1 SMALL JAR

3 lemons

135 g (4 ¾ oz) caster sugar

50 g (2 oz) unsalted butter

2 tablespoons cornflour

2 organic eggs

2 organic egg yolks

1. Mix the zest of three lemons with juice of two lemons and bring to the boil with the sugar and butter.
2. Strain the liquid.
3. Blend the cornflour with the juice from the remaining lemon. Stir into the warm liquid.
4. Beat the eggs and yolks and stir into the liquid, put the saucepan back on the heat and simmer, stirring constantly, until the curd thickens.
5. Pour into a clean jar or bowl and leave to cool.

raspberry sauce with vanilla

SERVES 4

90 g (3 ½ oz) caster sugar

150 ml (¼ pint) water

½ vanilla pod

180 g (6 ¼ oz) fresh or frozen raspberries

juice of 1 lime

2 tablespoons crème de cassis (optional)

1. In a stainless steel saucepan bring the sugar, water and the vanilla pod to the boil.
2. Add the raspberries and boil for about 5 minutes.
3. Add the lime juice and the crème de cassis.
4. Remove the vanilla pod and mix the sauce until smooth with a hand-held blender.
5. Strain the sauce through a fine sieve. Leave to cool.

granny-style vanilla sauce

SERVES 4

250 ml (8 fl oz) milk

½ vanilla pod

45 g (1 ¾ oz) caster sugar

4 organic egg yolks

40 g (1 ½ oz) cornflour

2 tablespoons unsalted butter, softened

100 ml (3 ½ fl oz) whipping cream

1. Halve the vanilla pod and scrape out the seeds. Bring the milk, vanilla pod and seeds to the boil in a saucepan. Remove the vanilla pod after the milk has boiled.
2. Beat the sugar, the egg yolk and the cornflour until white and fluffy.
3. Pour the hot milk into the egg mixture beating continuously.
4. Pour the mixture back into the saucepan and heat beating continuously. When the custard has thickened substantially, pour into a cold bowl.
5. Add the butter and beat into the warm custard.
6. Chill the custard in the refrigerator.
7. Whip the cream lightly and blend into the cream to make a fluffy vanilla sauce.

zabaglione

Zabaglione is a dessert made of egg yolks, sugar and sweet liqueur (usually Marsala), and sometimes cream and whole eggs. The zabaglione is a very light and airy custard, which is beaten to incorporate a lot of air. Zabaglione is traditionally served together with fresh dates. This custard is perfect together with any fresh berries or as a sauce to go with apple pie or crumble.

SERVES 4

4 organic egg yolks
90 g (3 ½ oz) caster sugar
150 ml (¼ pint) Marsala

1. Put all the ingredients in a stainless steel bowl over a pan of simmering water.
2. Beat until fluffy. You should see distinct marks from the whisk in the cream.
3. Remove the bowl from the pan carefully and continue to beat for about 1 minute until the cream has cooled a bit.

elderflower custard

This custard is a wonderful cake filling. It is also perfect as an accompaniment for cakes and pies, but you should use half the quantity of cornflour because you don't want the custard as thick.

MAKES ENOUGH FOR 1 CAKE

4 organic egg yolks
45 g (1 ¾ oz) caster sugar
2 ½ tablespoons cornflour
50 ml (2 fl oz) undiluted elderflower squash
300 ml (½ pint) whipping cream

1. Beat the egg yolks and the sugar until pale and fluffy.
2. Mix the cornflour with the elderflower squash.
3. Bring the cream to the boil and blend with the squash. Mix the warm liquid into the egg mixture.
4. Pour the custard back into the saucepan and simmer, beating until the custard has thickened. Leave to cool.

syrup

MAKES 1 SMALL BOTTLE

180 g (6 ¼ oz) caster sugar
100 ml (3 ½ fl oz) water
juice of 1 lemon

1. Bring all the ingredients to the boil,
2. Leave to cool and pour into a bottle or a bowl. Seal carefully.

classic chocolate sauce

The vegetable oil makes the finished sauce glossy. Always use good quality cocoa powder for sauces, desserts and cakes.

SERVES 4

50 g (2 oz) good quality cocoa powder
180 g (6 ¼ oz) caster sugar
150 ml (¼ pint) water
1 tablespoon vegetable oil

1. Mix together the cocoa powder, sugar and water. Boil for about 3 minutes.
2. Add the oil and either serve the sauce warm or leave to cool.

chocolate fudge sauce

SERVES 4

100 ml (3 ½ fl oz) milk
100 ml (3 ½ fl oz) whipping cream
40 g (1 ½ oz) brown sugar
50 ml (2 fl oz) golden syrup
1 teaspoon ground ginger
100 g (4 oz) milk chocolate
100 g (4 oz) good quality chocolate (70% cocoa solids)
1 tablespoon unsalted butter

1. Bring the milk, whipping cream, brown sugar, syrup and ginger to the boil. Leave to cool.
2. Chop the chocolate finely, then stir into the sauce together with the butter.

butterscotch sauce

Chill a plate in the freezer. Spoon a little sauce onto the plate to check the consistency. The longer you boil it, the thicker the sauce will be. Add lime zest or ground cardamom to give this classic sauce a modern twist.

SERVES 4

250 ml (8 fl oz) whipping cream
45 g (1 3/4 oz) caster sugar
100 ml (3 1/2 fl oz) golden syrup
1 teaspoon good quality cocoa powder

1. Let the ingredients boil for about 20 minutes in a heavy-bottomed saucepan. Leave to cool.

vanilla crème fraîche

When you buy vanilla pods you should look for soft, dark and juicy ones. The vanilla pods loose their aroma when they turn dry and hard. Store the pods in a dark, cool and airtight place to keep them fresh.

SERVES 4

300 ml (1/2 pint) crème fraîche
1/2 vanilla pod
2 tablespoons icing sugar

1. Whip the crème fraîche with an electric mixer until it is softly peaking.
2. Split a vanilla pod lengthways and scrape out the seeds. Mix the seeds with the crème fraîche.
3. Add icing sugar.

fromage blanc

SERVES 4

100 ml (3 1/2 fl oz) whipping cream
300 ml (1/2 pint) low-fat Greek yogurt
2 tablespoons icing sugar

1. Whip the cream until it is softly peaking.
2. Mix with the yogurt and add the icing sugar.

butterscotch cream

An easy shortcut is to buy ready-made fudge if you don't want to make your own.

SERVES 4

300 ml (1/2 pint) whipping cream
4 tablespoons cold butterscotch sauce,
    see recipe above

1. Whip the cream until fluffy and mix with the fudge sauce.

raspberry fool cream

SERVES 4

300 ml (1/2 pint) whipping cream
100 ml (3 1/2 fl oz) low-fat Greek yogurt
100 ml (2 fl oz) raspberries
2 tablespoons icing sugar

1. Whip the cream until softly peaking and mix with the yogurt.
2. Mash the raspberries lightly with the icing sugar.
3. Flavour the cream with the raspberries.

chocolate & raspberry marmalade

Sterilise jars before filling with jam or marmalade. Wash them thoroughly. Put them in the oven upside down on a wire rack at 120°C/250°F/gas 1/2 for about 30 minutes or plunge them into boiling water.

MAKES 1 JAR

225 g (8 oz) frozen raspberries
350 g (12 oz) muscovado sugar
75 g (3 oz) good quality dark chocolate
    (70% cocoa solids)

1. Simmer the raspberries and the sugar in a saucepan for about 15 minutes. Skim if needed.
2. Take the saucepan off the heat and melt coarsely chopped chocolate into the mixture.
3. Leave the marmalade to cool a bit before pouring into a sterilised glass jar and close the lid tightly.

rhubarb & ginger marmalade

Chill a small plate in the freezer. Spoon a little of the warm marmalade onto the chilled plate and push the marmalade with a spoon. It's ready if it won't run back straightaway.

MAKES 2 JARS
4 large rhubarb sticks
3.5 cm (1 ½ in) fresh root ginger
½ vanilla pod
juice of 1 lemon
50 ml (2 fl oz) water
1 kg (2 ¼ lb) preserving sugar
a few drops of red food colouring

1. Rinse and chop the rhubarb into small pieces, discarding any stringy bits. Slice the ginger thinly. Split the vanilla pod lengthways and scrape out the seeds.
2. Mix all the ingredients except the sugar in a heavy-bottomed saucepan and allow to boil uncovered for about 15 minutes.
3. Stir in the sugar, boil for a few minutes uncovered. Skimming if needed.
4. Remove the vanilla pod out and leave the marmalade to cool a bit. Colour the marmalade with a few drops of food colouring. Pour the marmalade into warm, sterilised jars and close the lids tightly.

strawberry jam

MAKES 2 JARS
900 g (2 lb) fresh strawberries
1 vanilla pod
1 tablespoon water
630 g (1 lb/6 oz) caster sugar
270 g (9 ½ oz) preserving sugar
zest and juice of 1 lime

1. Hull and halve the strawberries.
2. Split the vanilla pod lengthways and scrape out the seeds. Boil the strawberries for about 15 minutes together with the water and the vanilla seeds. Skim if needed.

3. Add the caster sugar, preserving sugar, lime zest and lime juice and bring to the boil.
4. Leave the jam to cool a bit before pouring it into warm, sterilised glass jars.

tomato & lemongrass marmalade

MAKES 2 JARS
1 kg (2 ¼ lb) organic tomatoes
3 stalks of lemongrass
zest and juice of 1 lemon
1 kg (2 ¼ lb) preserving sugar

1. Rinse and dice the tomatoes and put them in a saucepan.
2. Crush the lemongrass with the back of a knife to release the flavour.
3. Put the lemongrass in the saucepan together with the lemon zest and juice and boil, covered, for about 15 minutes.
4. Stir in the preserving sugar, boil uncovered for a few minutes. Skim if needed.
5. Take out the lemongrass and leave the marmalade to cool a bit. Pour into warm, sterilised glass jars.

blackcurrant jam

MAKES ABOUT 450 G (1 LB)
2 kg (3 ½ lb) blackcurrants
1 vanilla pod
1 tablespoon water
630 g (1 lb/6 oz) caster sugar
270 g (9 ½ oz) preserving sugar
zest and juice of 1 lemon

1. Rinse and pick the berries. Split the vanilla pod lengthways and scrape out the seeds. Put the berries in a saucepan with the water and vanilla seeds.
2. Boil uncovered for about 15 minutes and skim if needed.
3. Add the caster sugar, preserving sugar, lemon zest and lemon juice. Bring to the boil.
4. Leave the jam to cool a bit before pouring it into warm, sterilised glass jars.

sauces, creams & marmalades

sos in the kitchen

Why is the dough not rising?
- The liquid used in making the dough may have been too warm. If the liquid's temperature is over 38°C (100°F), there is a risk that the yeast will be killed, which will stop the dough from rising. (The temperature can be higher if you are using dry yeast.)
- The dough liquid may have been too cold, which is not actually wrong but will mean that the dough will take longer to rise. The advantage is that this gives the flavours longer to develop, so your bread will be tastier!
- The yeast may be too old. Don't forget to check the expiry date on the packet.
- The flour may have been too cold, which means the dough will take longer to rise. It is better to use flour at room temperature.
- The dough may be standing somewhere too cold or in a draft. Doughs like to be in a warm, even temperature where they can prove evenly. You can actually use this to control how fast the dough rises. Put the dough in a slightly cooler place if you want it to take its time, or a warmer place if you want to work faster.
- There may be too much flour in the dough, which makes it heavier and reduces its capacity to rise.

Why is the dough heavy instead of soft and elastic?
- If there is too much flour in the dough, it will become heavy and dense.
- The dough may have been kneaded for too long after the first rising. It often needs no more than one fold or two, depending on what type of bread you are baking.
- There may be insufficient salt. This makes it lifeless, reduces its capacity to prove and leaves it less springy.
- There may be too much fat or sugar in the dough. It will prove but will take longer than usual.

Why is the bread heavy instead of light and fluffy?
- The dough may not have been given long enough to rise. My rule of thumb is to let it double in size.
- The oven may have been too cold or the bread may not have been in for long enough, which will give a heavier bread. If the bread does have enough colour but still needs to be baked for longer, cover it with some kitchen foil so it can stay in a bit longer without burning.

Why are the rusks and biscuits so hard?
- There may not have been enough yeast or baking powder in the dough.
- There might have been too much sugar or too little butter in the dough.
- The rusks may have been cut up before they were cool enough. This can cause the edges to harden when they finally cool.

Why are the buns dry or hard?
- There may have been too much flour in the dough, which will make them dry.
- There may have been too little fat in the dough, which will also make them dry.
- The buns may not have been given long enough to prove on the tray, which could make them hard.
- The buns may have been in the oven for too long. Try raising the temperature and shortening the baking time.

Why is the cake bulging over the edge of the tin?
- The tin may be too small or was too full. It

should be no more than two-thirds full when you put it in the oven.

What made the sponge, muffins or scones chewy or rubbery?

- Never whisk flour into a mixture containing baking powder. This draws out the gluten, making the bread tough and dense.
- The flour may have been mixed into the batter for too long. Blend it in just enough to mix it evenly and no more.

What caused the cake to crack?

- The baking powder or bicarbonate of soda may not have been mixed evenly into the batter. Always mix baking powder or bicarbonate of soda into the dry ingredients before blending them into the mixture.
- There may have been too much flour added to the mixture.
- The oven may have been a bit too hot. Try a lower temperature next time.

Why has the cake stuck to the tin?

- The tin may not have been greased well enough. Try cooling the tin down with a damp tea towel. This should make it easier to loosen the cake from the tin.
- Let the cake cool down before trying to remove it from the tin.
- I generally use nonstick pans. I am careful to make sure that I always keep older tins greased with some cooking oil when they are not in use.

Why is the cake not rising?

- There may not be enough baking powder mixed in.
- The oven door may have been opened too often. Cakes need an even temperature to rise.
- The mixture may not have been whisked for long enough before the flour was added. Egg and sugar should be whisked up until fluffy and pale. Butter and sugar should be whisked until light and creamy.

- The mixture may have been stirred for too long after the flour and baking powder or bicarbonate of soda was added. This will reduce the cake's ability to rise.

Why did the fruit or berries sink to the bottom of the cake?

- The dough may have been too light to support the filling. Try rolling the fruit pieces or berries in a little flour before you add them to the mixture.
- Add a little more flour to the mixture next time.

Why is the biscuit dough crumbly?

- There may be too little liquid in the dough. Add a drop of water and the dough should bind together better.
- Some cookie doughs are supposed to be very dry, such as the dream cookies. You just need to squeeze the dough into small balls, which then flatten out on the baking tray.

Why is the biscuit dough so hard to roll out?

- Some doughs are tougher than others to roll out so it can be a good idea to roll a bit, have a break so the dough can rest and then have another go.
- There may be too much flour in the dough, making it dense and firm. Sprinkle some water on to the worktop, which gives the dough a better grip and makes it easier to roll out.
- There might be too little flour in the dough. Add a little extra flour and roll out on a well floured surface.

Why are the dream cookies so dense?

- The oven temperature may not have been quite right or the cookies may have been in for too long. If the oven is too warm, the cookies will get more colour. Ideally, they should stay pale and not be coloured at all.
- Smaller dream cookies need less time in the over; larger ones take longer.

Why are the biscuits becoming too flat on the baking sheet?

- Some biscuits should flatten and others not. Check the recipe and take a look at the picture to see how they should look.
- There may have been too much flour in the dough. If you have any dough left over, work a little more flour into the dough and try baking a couple of biscuits as a test.
- The oven may have been too hot. Try reducing the temperature next time.

Why is the cake or bread browning on the outside but is still not done on the inside?

- The baking tin may have been too high in the oven. Cover the cake or bread with some kitchen foil so it can stay in longer without burning.
- The cake or bread may have been in at too high a temperature for too short a time.
- The oven may have been too hot. Try reducing the temperature next time so the cake or bread can be in a little longer.
- If the bottom starts to burn, you can put an extra baking tray near the bottom of the oven to absorb some of the heat.

What is the difference between a conventional oven and a fan oven?

- A fan oven is more efficient and spreads the heat more evenly in the oven, which makes it ideal for baking. Bread is baked more evenly and rises better. A fan oven has a more powerful heating effect, which means that oven times may need to be reduced in some cases. I always bake my bread and cakes in a fan oven, so my recipes assume you are using one too. If you are using a conventional oven, you may need to increase the baking times slightly. Consult the manufacturer's handbook.

Why did the jam, squash or marmalade go mouldy or bubbly?

- You should never dip your finger into the boiled marmalade or jam because it will quickly go off if it comes into contact with saliva or bacteria.
- The berries you used may have been dirty or past their best. Take care to clean and rinse berries that are to be used for jam or squash.
- All the froth may not have been scooped off during boiling. The froth contains natural bacteria and fungi, which should be removed by scooping off the froth while boiling.
- The bottles or jars may not have been sterilised. Stand the empty bottles or jars upside down in an oven at 120°C/250°F/gas ½ or dip them into boiling water to sterilise them. Don't forget to sterilise the tops and caps too.
- The storage area may have been too warm. Jam and marmalade should be stored in a cool, dark place. Open containers need to be stored in a refrigerator.
- The jars or bottles may not have been closed tightly enough. Double check the lids.
- The boiling time may have been too short. Both jam and marmalade should be boiled for quite a while.

Why is the jam or marmalade so runny?

- If you used regular, granulated sugar there may not have been enough pectin in the fruit or the berries. You can mix regular sugar and preserving sugar together, fifty-fifty, for a thicker consistency.
- Some fruits and berries are high in pectin and so they jell more easily. Most fruits and berries need added pectin, however. Pectin can be added in a pure form or you can use special preserving sugar, which is pre-mixed with pectin.
- If the jam or marmalade is still too runny after a few days, bring to the boil again and use more pectin.
- The jam or marmalade may not have been boiled for long enough. If you boil for a little longer, the liquid will be reduced and the jam or marmalade will set more firmly.

kitchen magic

Yeast consists of living fungi which must be handled carefully if they are to do their job. The yeast transforms sugar into carbon dioxide through chemical and biological processes. This causes the dough to expand and rise, making it porous. You can use either fresh or dry yeast.

I always like to cook with fresh yeast and this is what has been specificed in the recipes. Fresh yeast must be stored in the fridge and used before the expiry date on the packet. Bear in mind that the liquid used in making the dough must not be over 38°C (100°F) or the yeast will die. The dough should be allowed to stand at room temperature in an even, draft-free space while it is rising.

Dried yeast is made from fresh yeast that has been dried and granulated. It is sold in 7 g sachets and does not need to be refrigerated. If substituting for fresh yeast in the recipes, work on the basis of using one sachet of dried yeast for every 500 g (about 1 lb) of strong plain flour. It should be mixed in with the flour rather than the liquid ingredients and the liquid used to make the dough should be warmer, around 50°C (122°F).

Easy-blend or fast-action yeast, which is widely available, is also available in 7 g sachets. Use one sachet of easy-blend or fast-action yeast for every 750 g (about 1 ½ lb) of strong plain flour. In general, you will need about twice as much fresh yeast as dried or easy-blend yeast, but this will vary according to the type of flour and the other ingredients. To avoid a strong, yeasty flavour, err on the side of caution and use less, rather than more, yeast and leave the dough to prove for longer.

Sourdough is made from water and flour, which gives the dough more flavour and more capacity to rise. It also gives a slightly chewier result. Many bread connoisseurs consider sourdough a must. It contains natural yeast and bacteria, which give a sour, fresh taste.

You can sometimes buy a cup of sourdough from a proper bakery. Keep it refrigerated in a jar, but take it out of the fridge the day before baking, or at least a few hours ahead. Dilute with water and flour until it goes thick, like a waffle batter. After a while, it will come to life and start bubbling.

Bicarbonate of soda is a naturally occurring substance that produces good, light cakes. It needs to be mixed with something acidic – like syrup or jam – to kick-off the expansion process. Then it works like yeast where carbon dioxide forms inside the dough or cake mixture, making it light and airy.

You can swap bicarbonate of soda for baking powder in the ratio of 1 teaspoon bicarbonate of soda to 2 teaspoons baking powder.

Baking powder is mix of bicarbonate of soda, acid salts and starch which is ideal for baking soft cakes and muffins. The expansion process begins before the cake is put in the oven. Store in an airtight container, otherwise it will not function properly.

recipe index

recipe index

tastes

tastes

A warm thank you to

Everyone who has contributed to this special baking book.

The Muffin Mafia, my mum and my grandmothers, but above all to my little sister Petronella for her helping hand with the baking, tasting and photographing.

Ulrika and Sten-Åke Magnusson for all your support and for letting me stay at your beautiful bed and breakfast "In my garden" in Mariefred. An extra special thank you to you, Ulrika, for helping out with the stage design at the photo-shoots.

Sweet little Ebba for tasting the high-hat cupcakes.

Photographer Wolfgang Kleinschmidt for all the beautiful pictures in the book and for your enthusiasm and creativity. www.kleinschmidt.se

Mikael Engblom for the perfect graphic design, which has led to another wonderful book. Mats Carlson for production management.

Tomas Ringqvist for the beautiful pictures on pages 8, 39, 73, 141, 142 and 198.

A Piece of Cake – Leila's Favourite Cakes and Breads is produced by Leilas Mat AB/ Leila Lindholm, www.leila.se. Previous books by the same author: *Leila's Dinner Tips* (2004) and *Leila's Food with a Golden Touch* (2006).

© Leila Lindholm
© English translation New Holland Publishers (UK) Ltd

This edition published in 2013.
Published in 2011 by New Holland Publishers (UK) Ltd
London   Cape Town   Sydney   Auckland
www.newhollandpublishers.com

Garfield House, 86–88 Edgware Road, London W2 2EA, United Kingdom
Wembley Square First Floor Solan Road Gardens Cape Town 8001 South Africa
Unit 1, 66 Gibbes Street, Chatswood, NSW 2067, Australia
218 Lake Road, Northcote, Auckland, New Zealand

Recipes, text and food styling: Leila Lindholm
Stage design: Ulrika Magnusson
Graphic design: Mikael Engblom
Photography: Wolfgang Kleinschmidt
Translator: Helena Thelander
Project manager, English translation: Chris Ward, Inkwell Foreign Rights
    and Translations
Copy editor, English edition: Lydia Darbyshire
10 9 8 7 6 5 4 3 2 1

ISBN 9781780094533

Printed and bound by Toppan Leefung Printing Ltd (China)

Keep up with New Holland Publishers on Facebook
www.facebook.com/NewHollandPublishers

£14.99